This book reveals how women have adopted the very traits the misogynists for centuries have accused them of having, and how this has given women both a means of power and a method for self-destruction. Accused by the misogynists of being sly and cunning, suspicious, prejudiced against other groups, aggressive, competitive, and rebellious, women adopted those very traits as a means of survival. These are the "Traits Due to Victimization" described by Gordon Allport.

Using the tools of the social psychologist, Nancy van Vuuren deals with these problems from a historical perspective. Her book will open a new area for research and evaluation The '70', she believes, should produce a special reform—expanding social history to include women.

The historical-social-psychological approach taken here gives the reader a seldom-found insight both into the status of women today and into the problems of the individual woman becoming a free person. For "unless the society, women and men, comprehends the subversion of women which has occurred, and which continues to occur, it will never deal with what has to happen for men and women to be liberated: sexism and sex discrimination must be ended in our social,

(Continued on back flap)

(Continued from front flap)

religious, political, economic, legal, and educational institutions."

In Section I, "The Subjugation of Women: A Judeo-Christian Tradition," Ms. van Vuuren looks at "some of the roles that women have adopted in the Western world over the past two thousand years, when mainly misogynist men controlled the economic, political, legal, and educational institutions."

Section II, "Witchcraft: A Threat to Church and State Supremacy," and Section III, "Sex: The Self-destructive Weapon," cover the "other" roles attributed to, and in fact played by, many women—magic/witchcraft and sex. "Magic/witchcraft," says Ms. van Vuuren, "cannot be separated from religion or from sex, for the purpose of magic/witchcraft is to control the supernatural and natural forces, and sex is always a part of this since sex can determine life, and death."

"But equality is necessary to freedom, to love, and to meaningful interpersonal relationships. And such equality can be achieved only by the combined action of those in the power structure and those who have been victimized and oppressed by that power structure."

How to accomplish this is the subject of the very practical tips given in the Conclusion of the book. Sensible, sane, well-reasoned, they are a far cry from the extremism of women's liberation fanatics. It is to be hoped that men and women both will hear and heed this clarion call to personhood for all.

THE
SUBVERSION OF WOMEN
AS PRACTICED BY CHURCHES, WITCH-HUNTERS, AND OTHER SEXISTS

by
Nancy van Vuuren

THE WESTMINSTER PRESS
Philadelphia

Book design by Dorothy Alden Smith

Published by The Westminster Press ®
Philadelphia, Pennsylvania

PRINTED IN THE UNITED STATES OF AMERICA

Library of Congress Cataloging in Publication Data

Van Vuuren, Nancy, 1938–
     The subversion of women as practiced by churches, witch-hunters, and other sexists.

     Bibliography: p.
     1. Woman—History and condition of women.
2. Woman—Social and moral questions. I. Title.
HQ1399.V35   301.41'2   73-5874
ISBN 0-664-20972-6

1781573

CONTENTS

FOREWORD

THE SUBVERSION OF WOMEN reveals how women have adopted
the very traits that the misogynists for centuries have accused
them of having, and how this has given women both a means
to power and a method for self-destruction. The traits that
misogynists claim women have are the "Traits Due to Victimization" described by Gordon Allport in *The Nature of
Prejudice*.

Our society still victimizes and subverts women. Most
women still bear the traits of oppressed people. Only full recognition of this fact by both women and men will make it possible for women, and so for men, to strive to be full, free, and
individual persons. But for this to happen, sexism and sex discrimination must be ended in our social, religious, political,
economic, legal, and educational institutions.

THE SUBVERSION OF WOMEN is written for those persons who
seek to understand the oppression of women in the past and in
the present as evidenced in social and religious values and
institutions, and who want to achieve the liberation of all persons. It is particularly directed to the individual woman seeking to understand herself and to be a person in her own right.

Every day we have further evidence that women are not
overcoming their oppression and that the society is not chang-

ing. The experiences of women's groups in and out of the feminist movement reveal the self-hatred and hatred of one's own group (in this case, women) which crops up regularly in individual women and in women's groups. Some organizations have dealt with this openly, but I am convinced that a knowledge of and an understanding of the Traits Due to Victimization are crucial to the liberation of the individual woman and to the survival of the women's movement as a movement for social change, for elimination of sexism in our society.

This book comes out of a myriad of life experiences, studies, and discussions. I want to acknowledge the women of the several feminist groups with which I have worked during the last four years, and the individual leaders in these groups with whom I have had many a long planning session and many discussions on group and "women" dynamics. These include Ina Braden, Ronnalie Howard, Alma Fox, Pat Roberts, Elizabeth Scott, Jody Raphael, Nancy Whitacre, and Edith Byrne. The person to whom I owe the deepest gratitude, however, is Richard Rieker, a man of deep commitment to the equality of all persons, which he carries into his daily life and his professional work. His extensive background in reading and experience provided an essential additional perspective. My daughter, Peta Marja, has shared her experiences as a child in a sexist society and thus has helped me to understand the early effects of sexism on children and their interactions with each other.

Thanks are also due to Diane McGill, Jacqueline Ramsey, and Mary Lou Rostosky for their assistance in typing the several drafts of the manuscript, and for their enthusiasm for the content of the book.

INTRODUCTION

The predominant role of woman conveyed throughout our society is that of providing for the man by cooking and cleaning, bearing his children, and giving him sexual satisfaction. The man's predominant role is outside the home, running industry, banks, the military, and earning the money that will pay for the expenses of the family's food, clothing, and home. The man's role is not perceived as that of making a home, assisting in the bearing and raising of children, or providing sexual satisfaction to the woman. The part of a man's life connected with living—wife, children, home, food—is considered secondary, since every man has these needs. What is secondary for the man is considered primary for the woman, because the values of the society define the woman as a secondary, inferior being.

This secondary/primary role of woman leaves her a nonperson. Bearing and raising children, cooking and serving meals, cleaning, washing and ironing, having sexual relations, does not give her much opportunity to be, or to feel that she is, a person. She has little opportunity for development or for self-expression. She, and *all* other women, are to be the same.

A startling example of how ingrained these role perceptions are is the expectation which young American men traveling to Europe today have that European women will give them food and lodging. And the expectation, on the whole, is correct. In this case the men do not have to "bring home" the money. The women provide everything.

No person can fulfill this role of woman without developing ego defenses. In *The Nature of Prejudice* (p. 157), Gordon Allport attempted to organize into a pattern the ego defenses that he had observed as Traits Due to Victimization:

Suffering from frustration
induced by discrimination and disparagement
leads to
sensitization and concern which

if the individual is basically extropunitive	if the individual is basically intropunitive
lead to	lead to
obsessive concern and suspicion	denial of membership in own group
slyness and cunning	withdrawal and passivity
strengthening in-group ties	clowning
prejudice against other groups	self-hate
aggression and revolt	in-group aggression
stealing	sympathy with all victims
competitiveness	symbolic status striving
rebellion	neuroticism
enhanced striving	

As Allport points out, these traits do not follow any particular pattern of domination, and each individual "victim" develops her or his own types and interrelationships of defenses. These ego defenses result from the interaction between the outside world and the individual's ego. Some patterns of interaction do appear, as we shall see in the coming chapters.

Together the outside world, the ego, the Traits Due to Victimization (the ego defenses), and the role models produce conflicting images of women. Nearly every advertisement shows the woman as sexy and lustful, or as a mother and wife. The sexy woman always has large breasts, a throaty voice, flirting eyes, and a seductive walk. All she expects, apparently, is to be looked at or to mouth some meaningless phrases about a deodorant or a shampoo. The woman who projects the mother image, on the other hand, is not sexy, nor is she intelligent, for she needs a man to tell her about timesaving products, soaps to get her laundry clean, and medicines to relieve her tension and headaches. The sex image and the mother image portrayed by the communications media reveal the woman as servant, her duty and desire being only to please men.

And, in fact, many women try desperately to play these conflicting roles. As they do this, though, they also take on many of the Traits Due to Victimization, mainly those of the intropunitive individual:

withdrawal and passivity

self-hate

in-group aggression (competition with other women for men, cattiness)

symbolic status striving

neuroticism

The descriptions of women given by the misogynists (including the communications media) include all the Traits Due to Victimization presented by Allport: Women gossip and tell secrets. They try to dominate men (threaten their masculinity). They are extravagant, and will take all that a man has (sexually, financially, etc.). Women are inferior and subordinate beings, lacking in intelligence, courage, and honesty, and can be grouped with the basest animals. They dress themselves up and decorate their faces in order to conquer men, and they tempt men to lust and so separate men from their God. Women are lustful, unchaste, adulterous. They are cunning and devious. Women deceive men.

Misogynous statements occur in nearly every piece of world-famous literature and every writing on philosophy and theology that raises the subject of women. For example:

Burke: "A woman is but an animal, and not an animal of the highest order."

Nietzsche: When a woman has scholarly inclinations, there is usually something wrong with her sexual nature. Yet, before marrying, one should always ask oneself: Can I stand this woman's conversation for the rest of my life?

Augustine: "Sex is degrading to the soul."

Chrysostom: "Women who deck themselves out in fine clothes entice men to lust."

Torquato Tasso: Every woman would wish to be a man, just as every deformed wretch would wish to be whole and fair, and as every idiot and fool would wish to be learned and wise.

Edgar F. Berman, M.D. (Committee on National Priorities, Democratic Party, U.S.A.): Physical factors, particularly the menstrual cycle and menopause, disqualify women for key executive jobs. "If you had an investment in a bank, you wouldn't want the president of your bank making a loan under these raging hormonal influences at that particular period." (*The New York Times,* July 26, 1970.)

When persons are told so often—by the media, by teachers, by writers—that these are their group characteristics, the persons tend to live up to the description, to what is expected of them. Robert Merton labeled this tendency "self-fulfilling prophecy." What people think of a person determines to a real extent what the person is. So if men—and men control business, advertising, education, the courts, the churches—say that women are sex objects, dangerous, unintelligent, etc., then women will tend to view themselves as sex objects, dangerous, unintelligent, etc., and will try to act accordingly. Perhaps the major discovery of the social psychologists in this regard is the recognition of the effect of *interaction* on a person's characteristics and traits. Allport goes so far as to state that "if we foresee evil in our fellow man [*sic*], we tend to provoke it; if good, we elicit it" (Allport, p. 156).

So, in looking at some of the roles that women have adopted in the Western world over the past two thousand years, when mainly misogynous men controlled the economic, political, legal, and educational institutions, we should expect to find roles that give evidence for the argument that women actually have the characteristics which the misogynists accuse them of having. We should also expect to find conflicts within the roles and within the women attempting to live out their perceptions of their roles.

A major force in the shaping of the institutions of the Western world was the Christian church. The Judeo-Christian tradition established men as the wielders of religious power. When the Roman Church became the predominant political institution, it forced its concept of and attitude toward women upon all other institutions. This is not to say that women had equality within earlier social, economic, and political institutions. Nevertheless, it is to say that the Roman Catholic Church, and later the Protestant Church, imposed its convictions of male supremacy and superiority on the entire Western world, and subverted women into the roles that men most feared, and so perhaps desired: sex and magic/witchcraft.

In order to comprehend this subversion, this undermining, and the resulting ego defenses revealed in the Traits Due to Victimization, we must first look at Christianity in historical perspective, paying particular attention to the attitudes toward women and the roles of women in the Christian churches. Here we shall see what the official positions were, and how women who attempted to meet the requirements, or who rebelled against them, took on by necessity the Traits Due to Victimization.

Having examined the attitudes toward women and the roles of women promulgated by the church and by church-dominated political, educational, legal, and economic institutions, we can look at the "other" roles attributed to, and in fact played by, many women—magic/witchcraft, and sex. Churchmen were preoccupied with both, which made magic/witchcraft and sex powerful tools for women to use to influence and manipulate men.

We shall find that generally the officially accepted religious women adopted the intropunitive traits, while witches and prostitutes revealed predominantly the extropunitive traits. But there were and are outspoken, aggressive, and cunning "religious" women, and there were and are witches and prostitutes who hate themselves and other women. The traits overlap and intermingle, as do the very roles in religion, magic/witchcraft, and sex.

Religion must include magic/witchcraft and sex, especially since it deals with supernatural powers, fertility, and creation. The sex roles are tinged with religious beliefs and attitudes and with magical beliefs. Magic/witchcraft cannot be separated from religion or from sex, for the purpose of magic/witchcraft is to control the supernatural and natural forces, and sex is always a part of this since sex can determine life, and death.

Different women have emphasized various aspects of these roles in religion, magic/witchcraft, and sex, but to be a "woman" in Western society has generally meant that one must fit oneself into one or more of these roles. When women have not been allowed to develop openly and equally, they have had to seek ways to manipulate those who outwardly held power, and they have done this through adopting the roles defined for them.

But equality is necessary to freedom, to love, and to meaningful interpersonal relationships. And such equality can be achieved only by the combined action of those in the power structure and those who have been victimized and oppressed by that power structure. To be able to do this, though, people —women and men—must first understand what has happened to them and to their society.

THE SUBJUGATION OF WOMEN:
A JUDEO-CHRISTIAN TRADITION

THE SUBJUGATION OF WOMEN: A JUDEO-CHRISTIAN TRADITION

1. Introduction

Despite the election of a woman as president of the National Council of the Churches of Christ in the U.S.A. in 1969, women still are not considered equal to men in the Christian churches. Only in 1970, for instance, did the Lutheran Church in America decide to allow women to become ministers. (By September, 1972, three women had been ordained.) The Roman Catholic and Anglican hierarchies still exclude women by canon law. By the time of its fall, 1973, meeting, the General Convention of the Episcopal Church, however, was ready to consider a resolution calling for the enactment of necessary legislation to remove all restrictions against women entering the priesthood. In 1971, the Catholic Seminary of Indianapolis had two women enrolled in the Master of Divinity program in preparation for the priesthood, but on September 13, 1972, the pope reconfirmed the papal veto against women priests. (In 1970, the Vatican refused to accept a West German diplomat because she was a woman.) And in 1972, Sally Priesand became the first woman rabbi.

The General Assembly of The United Presbyterian Church in the U.S.A. adopted several recommendations of the Task Force on Women at its May, 1972, meeting. These included:

A call for equal participation of women in writing any future confessional statements of the church, and in all future theological, ethical and ecclesiastical deliberations; a call for the initiation of a world-wide consultation planned by women on the development of women for full participation in the churches and social institutions; establishment of a Consulting Committee on Child Care and Development related to the new Program Agency; and a series of recommendations affirming women's right to the care and counseling of the church in regard to problem pregnancies and women's freedom of choice concerning the completion or termination of those pregnancies. (*Monday Morning,* July, 1972, p. XIV.)

Many of the churches are striving to understand human sexuality and to incorporate this understanding into their theology and practices. But the religious in the Roman Catholic Church are still celibate. Priests are warned in their training about women, and are told never to be alone with a woman. The religious orders in the Lutheran, Anglican, and Methodist churches also require celibacy, though the ministry of the non-Roman churches do not.

When so much emphasis and value are placed upon celibacy, particularly celibacy of the male, then women are perceived as, and therefore are even more purely, sex objects. The man deprived of his sexuality is more aware of sex than the man whose sexuality is one part of his relationship with another person. The woman as sex object threatens the celibate man's "spirituality."

What is even more important than the fear of women and the perception of them as sex objects by the male church hierarchies is the total lack of knowledge and understanding of women as persons through personal experience. The unknown is always frightening. The fear and sexual perception cannot be overcome except through knowledge and experience.

Fear of open discussion of human sexuality, of the sexuality of all persons, and opposition to "sex education" in the schools expressed by several churches reveal further the difficulties many church people have with their own sexuality.

The characteristics of the oppressed can be found in women in the Christian churches. The majority of churchwomen try to be passive and withdrawn, and helpful servants, since this is the role set out for them, as proof that they have overcome the evil powers naturally within women. They also express self-hate and aggression against their own group—Allport's "intropunitive" traits. Those women who refuse to accept these traits and who seek power tend to develop traits of slyness and cunning, of manipulation—Allport's "extropunitive" traits.

2. Biblical Times and the Church Fathers

The Middle East has a long history of subjugating women. Whereas the agricultural societies had female goddesses, oracles, and warriors, both in mythology and in practice, the pastoral societies had male-dominated myths and a patriarchal society, based on tribal groups.

In the tribes of Israel the oldest man had authoritarian power. He could order his sons and daughters at will, and he could use his daughter-in-law as he would. The society had no place for the single woman. If a woman did not marry, her father exercised control over her until he died. If she did marry, her father had to pay a dowry to the man who took her. If the father could not pay a dowry, he might sell her as a slave.

The widow had few rights in the law of ancient Israel, and had a limited livelihood. Woman's value lay in her producing a son who would carry the name and property of his father and of the tribe. Therefore, the law provided that a widow should marry the next oldest son of her husband's family and the first child should carry the dead man's name.

The bearing of children, especially of sons, took top priority in ancient Israel. The story of Abraham and Sarah illustrates this: Sarah took a concubine for Abraham in order for him to have a son, leaving the concubine as a "nonmother," and when Sarah conceived in her old age, this was viewed as her present for serving God. At that time, sexual purity was not as important as having children. And the mother of the child was not as important as the father. As with the child of the concubine, the mother might have no rights to the child.

Kings and rich men generally either had several wives or had concubines. The wife might even give her husband a concubine in order to maintain some influence over him. The main duty of the wife was to keep the household, make the husband happy, and raise the children—bearing them, too, if possible. The sexual satisfaction of the husband, not of the wife, was considered important and worth the purchase of women who under the purchase agreement would have few rights or privileges, and would have short-lived security.

As in most societies, the poor in Israel had little freedom. Everyone worked; everyone lived together; everyone had responsibility for the children. No one could readily break out of this existence, but a woman could find a tenuous place in another economic group through marriage, or by becoming a concubine.

Perhaps the best expression of the power that men had over women, even when they married them, is the Tenth Commandment:

> You shall not covet your neighbor's house; you shall not covet your neighbor's wife, or his manservant, or his maidservant, or his ox, or his ass, or anything that is your neighbor's. (Ex. 20:17.)

The commandment is not directed to women at all, since they did not have the freedom to obey or disobey the commandment. The wife was grouped with the servants, the animals, and other property.

Another expression of this power was the legal right of the father or the husband to prevent any vow made by the daughter or wife to stand. When the man made a vow, it stood. (Num. 30:2.) A widow or a divorcée, however, could make a vow for herself, though it is difficult to imagine that she could implement a vow so long as she was dependent upon her father or her father-in-law for survival.

This type of situation existed in the pre-small-farm period and in the industrial period. When two persons married and owned property or a plot of farmland, they worked the farm together, and the widow could continue to gain a living from the land. Such a situation, however, appears to have been unusual for societies described in the Old Testament.

What did women do to survive within this context? Some manipulated each other and the men whose attention, power, and property they wished to gain. They seduced men. They connived against wives and concubines.

Deborah served as a judge of Israel and led the nation to the defeat of Sisera, the Canaanite captain. Jael, the wife of Heber, deceived Sisera by appearing to wait on him and serve him, and then she drove a tent peg into his temple.

Women served as the spoils of war, and so as the pawns of the society—and also as spies. And no spy is trusted, abroad or at home.

Delilah tricked Samson into revealing the source of his strength, his hair, which she then cut off when he was asleep.

Jezebel flaunted herself and caused men to pay for touching her.

Women were not allowed to fight as warriors. Death at the

hands of a woman was considered the worst kind of insult. And so when Abimelech, while leading the forces against Schechem, was hit over the head with a millstone by a woman, he ordered his armor-bearer to slay him so that "Men say not of me, A woman slew him" (Judg. 9:51–54).

But women chose their heroes. For instance, after David killed Goliath, the women greeted King Saul singing, "Saul has slain his thousands, and David his ten thousands" (I Sam. 18:7). And Saul was angry and jealous of David.

Here also appears the recurring theme of threatened manhood. Saul must prove his power and kingship by killing more than David and thus receive the praise of women. But David disparages this attention and love of women. Upon the death of Saul and Jonathan, he tells the women to "weep over Saul, who clothed you in scarlet, with other delights; who put ornaments of gold upon your apparel" (II Sam. 1:24), while he speaks of his love for and from Jonathan which passes the love of women (v. 26).

In Proverbs 31:3 a mother tells her son not to give his strength, presumably through sexual intercourse, to women. She also refers to the scarcity of the virtuous woman whom the husband can trust, who will do him good and not evil, who will work hard with her hands spinning and sewing. Such a woman will make fine linen and sell it and will deliver girdles to the merchant while her husband sits among the elders. She will run the household efficiently and have the respect of her children. This virtuous woman must not receive favor, for it is deceitful; or be beautiful, for beauty is vain.

A woman in Old Testament times could not bear the sign of the covenant because she could not be circumcised. She had to strive to make up for this lack, which is the physical lack of a penis—later the source for Freud's accusation that women have "penis envy." A woman fails spiritually under the Old Law because she is a woman. So woman, inferior creature, still had to try to prove her virtue, and the Old Testament proof of blessedness was the bearing of a male child—conceived only through sexual intercourse.

It would appear from Old Testament warnings that women did manipulate men into marrying them. No wonder, when marriage was the only means by which a woman could gain economic security. But even this security was tenuous, especially when the man had several wives. Esther, for instance, became queen only when the king decided he wanted her more than Queen Vashti, who was acting "uppity." The eunuchs who were in charge of the wives and concubines also exercised much power over the women and had to be manipulated in order for a woman to gain attention, wealth, or power.

Prostitution was rampant in the urban areas of ancient Israel. According to Proverbs 6:26, the prostitute could be bought "for a loaf of bread." The author of Proverbs recommends the use of the prostitute as opposed to becoming involved with a woman:

> Do not desire her beauty in your heart,
> and do not let her capture you with her eyelashes.
> (Prov. 6:25.)

The warning is given especially against adultery, which is paralleled to stealing property. Another reference to prostitution is made in Proverbs 9:13–18, where the prostitute who sits at the high places of the town is described as calling to those who pass by, saying:

> Stolen water is sweet,
> and bread eaten in secret is pleasant.
> (Prov. 9:17.)

Under these conditions women developed roles bearing various Traits Due to Victimization:

Withdrawal and passivity

Self-hate
In-group aggression
Sympathy with all victims
Neuroticism
Obsessive concern and suspicion
Slyness and cunning
Prejudice
Aggression and revolt

and the misogynists used these traits or characteristics as the basis for more oppression.

The coming of the Messiah did not liberate women. God became definitely male in *his* incarnation, Jesus, and he used the body of a woman to allow himself to become incarnate. Without sexual intercourse, God caused a birth which, in hindsight, was considered a miracle. (It is worth mentioning here that young Greek women frequently said that they conceived their first child out of wedlock with a "god.") Thus Mary became the mother of Jesus, God incarnate, the highest position any woman could attain. The fact that the Christians had to believe that the incarnation of God occurred without any sexual experience suggests how important the relationship between celibacy and godliness had become.

Jesus surrounded himself with men, according to the Bible, and never had a personal friendship or sexual contact with a woman. He did take note of particular women, though, and was sympathetic to them, responding to them as persons. But these women tended to be those who professed guilt and sin for sexual drives or women who served men. Nevertheless, Jesus did speak to and of women as children of God, capable of belief and of knowing the Word of God.

Apparently women were among the first "consecrated" church leaders and officials. Women assisted in teaching and converting people. Several disciples sought women to work among the people. Many women, ministers, provided shelter and assistance to the poor. Phoebe (Rom. 16:1) was the first deaconess officially recorded.

Women prophets proliferated (see Acts 2:17–19; 21:9; I Cor. 11:5). In fact, their enthusiasm and dynamism may have frightened men such as Paul. In his letter to the Corinthians, Paul directs the people how to act and speak in church:

> Let your women keep silence in the churches: for it is not permitted unto them to speak; but they are commanded to be under obedience, as also saith the law. And if they will learn any thing, let them ask their husbands at home: for it is a shame for women to speak in the church. . . . Let all things be done decently and in order. (I Cor. 14:34–35, 40.)

In his letter to Timothy, Paul states that women should dress modestly:

> with shamefacedness and sobriety; not with braided hair, or gold, or pearls, or costly array; but (which becometh women professing godliness) with good works. Let the woman learn in silence with all subjection. But I suffer not a woman to teach, nor to usurp authority over the man, but to be in silence. (I Tim. 2:9–11.)

Paul goes on to note that Adam was formed first, and that not Adam but the woman was deceived and so was in transgression. "Notwithstanding, she shall be saved in childbearing, if they continue in faith and charity and holiness with sobriety." (I Tim. 2:15.) Paul also states that a bishop can have only one wife.

Paul, perhaps, was particularly concerned that men spend their time praying instead of enjoying their bodies. His way of assuring this was to end their association with women, placing the full responsibility on women, which was the practice of the times.

Obviously Paul was not describing the position of women even in the church, but was suggesting that women be excluded further and that they should bear guilt for all intimate interpersonal relationships. He was defining a rule that was not followed or even adopted until the development of the nuclear middle-class family in the sixteenth century. Nevertheless, it is important to note his attitudes, for his letters were influential in the development of the attitudes toward women in the Christian churches. After all, *his* letters, not those of a feminist, were preserved (even if by chance) and used as church authority.

In speaking of widows, whose plight was a cause for concern throughout the Bible, Paul suggests that the widow would be saved if she prayed night and day; but if she lived in pleasure, she would be dead while she lived. The believer must provide for *his* family. But, Paul continues:

> Let a widow be enrolled if she is not less than sixty years of age, having been the wife of one husband; and she must be well attested for her good deeds, as one who has brought up children, shown hospitality, washing the feet of the saints, relieved the afflicted, and devoted herself to doing good in every way. But refuse to enrol younger widows; for when they grow wanton against Christ, they desire to marry, and so they incur condemnation for having violated their first pledge. Besides that, they learn to be idlers, gadding about from house to house, and not only idlers but gossips and busybodies, saying what they should not. So I would have younger widows marry, bear children, rule their households, and give the enemy no occasion to revile us. For some have already strayed after Satan. (I Tim. 5:9–15.)

Not giving the enemy occasion to "revile us" appears to have been a major concern for Paul. The widows were viewed by Paul as a special order (perhaps ordained) in the church. These widows performed the functions of the deaconesses. There were also widows, however, who received alms and showed their gratitude by praying for the community.

In contrast to the above quotations, Acts, ch. 17:4, tells of Paul's attempts to convert the chief women in Thessalonica. In his letter to the Philippians, Paul asks them to help the women who "labored with me in the gospel" (Phil. 4:3). Paul baptized Lydia, a seller of purple. He commanded the spirit of divination to leave another woman, apparently a prostitute, thus preventing her masters from making their profit. The author of Acts states that Paul was punished by the magistrates for doing this, but says nothing about what happened to the woman who had lost her means of living, or about the exploitation of women generally. (Acts 16:14–24.)

The Bible, then, between the roles of women it describes and the attitudes toward women it conveys, expresses a fear of women and a limited recognition of women as persons. In this process the authors of the Bible impute to women traits of the oppressed, saying that women are sly, cunning, aggressive, and deceptive. If a woman is good, she is so because she has overcome all the bad natural traits of women and has adopted ego defenses characteristic of the intropunitive Traits Due to Victimization.

The church fathers tended to follow Paul's lead.

Tertullian in the second century spoke vehemently against marriage and severely criticized women who adorned themselves with any kind of decoration, such as jewelry. He said that women only debase men and lead them from their spiritual concerns. The female sex is "the devil's gateway." Every woman is an Eve, the carrier of lust, the one who yields to the temptation of the serpent.

Clement of Alexandria stated, "Every woman should blush at the thought of what she is."

Augustine condemned all sexual relations as degrading to the soul.

Chrysostom stated, "Among all the wild beasts, there is none more harmful than woman." He also denounced women for dressing themselves so as to attract men and to make them lust.

Jerome accused woman of being the true Satan, "the foe of peace, the subject of dissension, and only her absence assures tranquillity." Jerome opposed marriage; but if a man did not heed this advice, he should, at least, avoid sexual intercourse as much as possible.

Origen of Alexandria conducted his own "nunnery," where he took women from some of the best Roman families to teach them doctrine and to help them to live "Christian" lives. According to Eusebius, because Origen was working so intimately with women, he had himself made a eunuch to avoid suspicion. Even though he worked closely with women, Origen does not mention women as being as righteous as men or as carrying out the work of God.

When Constantine became Christian very few other citizens of the Roman Empire were also Christian. And as Christianity became the state religion, all that citizens had to do was to change the outer format for their religious expression. And if later studies of the worship of Priapus are anywhere near correct, the old pagan religions continued for at least seventeen hundred years under the guise of Christianity. (Cf. Richard Payne Knight, *A Discourse on the Worship of Priapus and Its Connection with the Mystic Theology of the Ancients,* and Thomas Wright, *The Worship of the Generative Powers During the Middle Ages of Western Europe;* both, The Julian Press, Inc., 1957.) The concern of many Christians to wipe out the pagan religions apparently was a major motivating force for the emphasis on celibacy in the church. This in turn guaranteed a preoccupation with sex in the church.

The church fathers supported the developing male hierarchy and the authoritarian decision-making. The more prestige became associated with church positions, the more women were excluded. Then at the height of the disruptions of Roman society by the "barbarian" invasions, religious men grouped together into monasteries and built up an independent economic and political existence, first in the local vicinity, later spreading to larger and larger geographical areas. A hierarchy of power was developed that eventually excluded women more completely than had the militaristic Roman Empire.

For women, the value placed upon virginity as opposed to childbearing had begun to increase during New Testament times. By the third century, women were making a public profession of chastity, whereas earlier the vows were made in private to the bishop and the woman continued her life with her parents or family.

During these early centuries it is possible that Christians lived in communal groups, or at least in neighborhoods, and assisted in the economic support of each other. Religious women most probably were a part of this. But many women, as did many men, became hermits, or anchoresses. For them, clearly, virginity was essential.

From the public professions of chastity and the acts of martyrdom came the hagiography of the female saints which regularly emphasized that the woman was a virgin. Then, through being a virgin, the woman was able to exercise supernatural powers, speak of God, or endure terrible pain or suffering. The key point of the hagiography is that to be godly, the woman must be a virgin. (If the woman did not take a vow of chastity, then her highest value was to bear many children.)

In early documents of the church written by women, the author is referred to first as "Virgin." For example, the fourth-century writer Etheria is listed as "Etheria, Virgin from Galicia," author of *A Pilgrimage to the Holy Places of the East.* There is no such emphasis for men, and apparently "virginity" was *not* the usual state of men in the church.

In writing about the pilgrimage, Etheria reveals herself as a well-educated woman, for she writes in detail about the meth-

ods of worship, the places, and the people. She constantly reminds the reader that men are in control by her references to
the bishops, monks, and priests who conduct all the ceremonies
and tours. Probably Etheria was of a wealthy family, for otherwise she would not have had the time or the money to attend a
tour, and would not have had the education to be able to write
the description. We are left wondering, however, who educated her, who paid for it, and why—and how many other
women there were like her and how they lived.

In contrast to these developments within Christianity, the
Germanic tribes depended upon the work of women for survival. And the pagan fertility rites honored women as well as
men. Here again the agricultural society provided a healthier
economic role for women, which in turn allowed women to develop self-respect. (We shall see parallels of this in the convents.) Women in the rural society were not denied contact
with the supernatural. In fact, as in ancient Greece, women
frequently became the seers, the oracles, the astrologists, and—
in Christian terms—the witches. Women were viewed as the
key means, on many levels, for the continued existence of the
tribe.

As kingdoms and fiefs developed, lineage became the decisive factor in political power. The blood heritage and the name
held precedence over the sex. Generally the male child was first
in line, but the female child also had her place. This emphasis
led to women as well as men ruling over tribes and over geo-
graphic areas.

3. The Middle Ages and Heretical Movements

The Bible and the church fathers present a limited perspective
and deal with the events and concerns of a small group of

people. Once Christianity spread throughout the Roman Empire, the conflicts and interpretations became more diffuse. The early history of the church, in the sense of investigating what people believed and how they adapted their "pagan" rites to Christianity, has never been written. Church historians, philosophers, and theologians have neglected the people.

During the Middle Ages the church became an institution concerned with wealth and power. Within this context, and as a male hierarchy, the Roman Church could not accept the secular emphasis on lineage. The more the church, especially Pope Gregory, attempted to implement celibacy, the more it opposed the family as the means of determining succession to power. When priests could not have legitimate children and yet were bound on the path of this worldly power, they could never accept the secular procedures for maintaining control over the throne. Lineage, therefore, provided the context for much of the power struggle between church rulers and secular rulers. The church claimed that its hierarchy should rule because it had the power of God. The secular rulers established power by family and claimed their superiority. Eventually the two united in the concept of the divine right of kings.

Women were usually left out of this power struggle except as wives, mistresses, and mothers, and as they happened to fall into the line of succession, which only increased the opposition of the church to the secular power. How could a woman be stronger and have more authority than the church?

During the Middle Ages as the church developed its organization and its economic and political power, many men in the nobility used the church as the means to success. The church controlled all education, and educated mainly men. But when a woman was in line for power, the family made sure she received a good education. In some cases a priest would teach such women. In others, men who did not take orders would become tutors to noble families. Yet the most frequently used means in the late Middle Ages for a noblewoman to be educated was the convent. In many ways the convent made economic and political power possible for women, just as the monasteries did for men.

Women probably began to live together in communities in the early apostolic period. Scholastica, Benedict's sister, formed an order for women and established a rule early in the sixth century. By the late Middle Ages, kings and queens were forming nunneries, to which the queen might retire after, and sometimes before, her husband's death. Noblewomen and daughters of knights and nobles would frequently board at the convent or become nuns. If a woman's husband was to be away for an extended time, she would live at the convent. Noble families would keep daughters in convents until the proper marriages were arranged. Women who could not be married, for whatever reason, would most likely become nuns and give their dowries to the convent. In some cases this meant a child of twelve taking vows for life. The convent became the protection, and the alternative, for the aristocratic woman or female child.

Most convents also had poor sisters, women of the village. The same economic and social class structure prevailed within the convents as without. Although technically anyone could organize a convent, the pattern was for someone with money to set it up and to maintain control. The convents provided the means for the economic survival of women, and in many cases made possible the wealth, power, and influence of women. By pooling their resources, their abilities, and their labor, they could become independent (as a whole) and self-sufficient.

The convents and the monasteries might be viewed as the precursors of the town, of urban industry, and of trade fairs and merchants. In England convents would own and run large farms, employing male and female villeins for harvesting. Individual convents or groups of convents in a particular locale became famous for their wool, their wines and liqueurs, their linens, scents, and embroidery, their sweets and ices—the last mainly in Italy and Sicily.

1781573

The abbesses of Quedlinburg in the Harz Mountains were princesses of the Holy Roman Empire, which meant they had a vote in the German diet and a seat on the bench of the Rhenish bishops. (During the Reformation they became Lutherans and lost their feudal sovereignty and most of their estates.) The abbess of Las Huelgas de Burgos in Spain was a princess palatine, having complete power over her serfs and being responsible only to the queen. She had the power to license and to suspend priests and confessors, to make decisions of law, and to direct all religious practices in the area. The abbess herself heard confessions and gave absolution. She was ordained in sacred vestments and miter. The abbesses of San Benedetto in Italy were also installed with miter, pastoral staff, gloves, and ring. Pope Pius V upheld their power. The abbesses of Barking, Wilton, Shaftesbury, and St. Mary, Winchester, in England, ranked as baronesses. Several abbesses ruled monasteries that included both men and women.

For the noblewoman the convent might provide the mechanism for power which she could not exercise on her own outside the convent. This very aspect of the medieval convents made the male bishops nervous. Consistently the male hierarchy tried to contain, control, and cloister the nuns. And consistently, during this period, the women refused to comply and went on about their work.

The aristocratic abbesses and nuns were frequently the subject of complaints and reprimands, mostly for wearing fine clothes and dressing in a manner "unbecoming nuns." In 1441, for example, the prioress Clemence Medford at Ankerwyke, in Buckingham, England, was complained of for wearing gold rings and silk veils. The bishop criticized the nuns at Elstow, in Bedfordshire, England, for wearing too colorful and too revealing clothes. A prioress was accused of wearing expensive furs and silk and of keeping company with a John Munkton.

Aristocratic women in the medieval period usually received an academic education to prepare them in the event that chance should place them in power. Aristocratic nuns similarly intended to be educated and to educate. The male hierarchy did not approve. Innumerable times bishops forbade nuns to teach, and forbade convents to have children reside and study there, especially male children. Even the Rule for Nuns written in A.D. 512 by Caesarius of Arles specifically denied nuns the right to educate or rear children. Nevertheless, the nuns carried on. Usually the children involved were relatives of the nuns, placed in an individual nun's care. Sometimes the money derived from keeping the children helped the convent to survive.

All the convents had regular religious routines, more or less stringent, depending upon the rule and the individuals involved. The church hierarchy was threatened by the organization and the power of the women in some of the convents and intended to prevent them from rivaling the monks for power in church and state. (Many bishops were equally threatened by the monasteries.)

The thirteenth century brought the first official church regulations for nuns, and in 1298 Pope Boniface VIII issued the bull *Periculoso* to force all religious women to be cloistered. Religious women were to be neither seen nor heard. No nun was to leave the cloister and no person was to visit. The bishop was to enforce this rule. The women, as before, generally did not comply.

One must remember the difficult position of the aristocratic women during medieval times. There were no police, not even nations or national armies. When one baron fought another, the greatest punishment for the loser was for "his" women to be raped. They were the spoils of war. Women were not mercenaries or knights. Aristocratic women in particular had no means of defense. The peasant woman at least might have a pitchfork, though when a village was overrun or plundered, the only hope for the woman was that of hiding.

The nuns found that by living together they were safer than when alone, but periodically the convents themselves were sacked and the nuns raped. Apparently the virginity of nuns was a great fascination for the men—channeled into religious terms in the church, but providing again a preoccupation with the sexual being of women.

As commerce developed and cities grew, the measure of wealth shifted from land to goods that could be sold for money. Agricultural workers became factory workers, and a new urban society came into existence. The nuclear family appeared, as did the wage economy. Both men and women began to work outside the home in order to earn money with which to purchase food and clothing and to rent a place to live.

In the fourteenth century the church fell into schism. Even the superficial unity of the church and its power dissolved. The schism convinced more and more of the persons who opposed the influence of the church that it was completely corrupt. The conciliar movement grew and demanded that the councils of the church have power over the clerical hierarchy. The councils, which represented a broader spectrum of the population but still not the poor or women, thought they could reform the church and return it to its original state.

The people—the peasants and the tradespeople—had never become Christians by theological measures. The majority of priests during the Middle Ages had not even been able to read the Latin of the Mass. It is no wonder that with the development of a commercial economy and urban living, traditional interpretations of doctrine were questioned and opposition to the ruling hierarchies increased. Hence the rise of "heretical" movements across Europe. I use "heretical" here in the same manner as did the medieval popes, meaning anyone who refused to obey the existing religious power structure. Even the new monastic movements, such as that of Francis of Assisi, were constantly on the verge of being proclaimed heretical, since they wanted to make the church more "Christlike," according to their own interpretations.

Yet Francis of Assisi did not consider women as part of the "people of God." He called only men to join the Friars Minor in the thirteenth century, and he described the Rule as being

to observe the Holy Gospel of our Lord Jesus Christ, by living in obedience, without property and in chastity. (Colman J. Barry, *Readings in Church History*, Vol. I, p. 417; The Newman Press, 1960. Copyright © 1960 by The Newman Press.)

And men were to be accepted into the order if they believed in the Catholic faith and the Sacraments of the church:

And if they believe all these things, and if they will confess them faithfully and observe them firmly to the end, and if they have no wives, or, if they have and their wives have already entered a monastery, or have, with the authority of the diocesan bishop, given them permission after having made a vow of continency, and if the wives be of such an age that no suspicion may arise concerning them, let them (the ministers) say to them the word of the Holy Gospel, that they go and sell all their goods and strive to distribute them to the poor. If they should not be able to do this, their good will suffices. (Barry, Vol. I, p. 418.)

Later on, in the Second Rule, Francis of Assisi gave specific instructions with regard to association of the brothers with women.

I strictly command all the brothers not to have suspicious intimacy, or conferences with women, and let none enter the monasteries of nuns except those to whom special permission has been granted by the Apostolic See. And let them not be godfathers of men or women, that scandal may not arise on this account among the brothers or concerning the brothers. (Barry, Vol. I, p. 420.)

Clare, however, an Italian nun and devotee of Francis of Assisi, took the vow of poverty in the early thirteenth century and formed the order of Franciscan nuns, the Poor Clares (the Second Order). Francis later founded the Third Order, or Tertians, for persons who wanted to live by a rule in the world. This order included communities of men and communities of women.

Francis of Assisi had disagreed with the church as it existed, but his means to correct it did not allow equal participation by women. Sex (virginity and chastity) continued to be a major issue in the church. The religious must have no sexual relations.

Indirectly, this emphasis by Francis of Assisi reveals what use had been made of women by some priests and monks of the church during the Middle Ages. The concubines and mistresses of ancient Israel had never disappeared.

Celibacy resulted in the oppression of women, mainly on two levels. The most devastating level was that of the difference between belief, or definition of godliness, and action. The woman who became the mistress of the celibate could have no respect, no acceptable role in the society. The celibate might even have to conceal her and their relationship. The second level was the training given the celibate, warning him to stay away from women, not to talk with women, not to have any feelings or personal concerns for women. One might ask what the value or godliness of celibacy could be if such rigid rules, which placed over half the population outside the understanding and concern of the church hierarchy, were necessary.

Reformers, such as Francis of Assisi, had every intention of eliminating the first level of oppression, that of talking about celibacy but having mistresses. The second level was intended to be the means to eliminating the first.

To some reformers and sects the involvement of clergy and religious with women was disgraceful. The purpose of women should not be sexual pleasure, but the bearing of children. As Jerome said, one should not rush into intercourse, even when married. The godly do not involve themselves in sexual desires. Yet many of the reformers married, including Martin Luther and even Thomas Cranmer, who brought his wife across the Channel in a trunk before he became archbishop of Canterbury during Henry VIII's schism with the church in Rome.

Women flocked to the reform movements. These women must have been of the urban lower and middle class. The peasant woman still had a position in the rural family through her labor and through the emphases on fertility and various forms of magic and pagan rites.

During this period the merchant guilds developed for themselves a place within the church and the urban society. The urban areas also provided the core for the "heretical" movements from the twelfth century on. The merchant guilds, though, tended to support the *status quo* and maintained careful controls over their members. The townsmen who could not join the guilds, such as the weavers, seem to have formed the core of the heretical movements, which worked against the guilds and their patron, the church. The weavers were the first to be caught by the instability of the economy, while the guilds could relax or tighten their membership in order to maintain a somewhat stable market and price. The weavers, without such stability, resented the position of the guildsmen and their power and wealth.

Among the weavers were women, a fact not readily recognized by historians. In the urban household everyone had to work if anyone was to survive. The majority of city dwellers were very poor. Weaving was a job which from the twelfth to the fifteenth centuries, the prefactory period, could be done at home, so it frequently fell to women. All the weavers were at the mercy of the farmers who produced the wool and the male-merchants who received the profits.

As might be expected, then, women also formed a major portion of the flagellant groups which moved across Western Europe in the later Middle Ages. They proclaimed the coming of the millennium, the utopia, when all persons would be free and equal. The flagellants beat themselves, sometimes literally to a pulp, in the village square, calling for salvation. Again, these appear to have been persons mainly from urban areas who were constantly on the border of starvation and unemployment. The existing church meant nothing to them. The intellectual reform movements had no effect upon them. They wanted to change the entire society, and so they took the road of religious revolution to try to overthrow the unjust system of wealth and power.

Several individuals and groups opposed the wealth of the church. Women could particularly respond to this general opposition, for most of the benefices and the tithes went to men, yet women had to pay tithes out of meager incomes, out of the food they needed for their families. The church did little for the urban poor who lived in filth, hunger, among rats, and in the midst of disease and plague. And the men of the church, too, would father children and leave the women to head and support the family. No welfare or unemployment programs, not to mention child care, existed to make life more bearable.

According to Norman Cohn in *The Pursuit of the Millennium,* the woman also provided the emotional force for Anabaptism and for the overthrow of the power of local bishops and priests. To achieve this, many women proclaimed themselves as having special powers. Such proclamations, which set persons above the hierarchy of the church, were bound to be termed heretical, and led to the extensive persecutions and executions of "heretics" from the thirteenth century on. Since no legal processes had to be followed, any person displeasing to the local cleric could be condemned. Women received the full brunt of the attack, for an outspoken woman could easily be declared a heretic or a witch. Several heretical movements involved women as preachers and as carriers of the Word of God, similar to the Christian community of the first century A.D. The Waldenses, for instance, who sent women and men all over France preaching "contempt for ecclesiastical power," claimed to hold power from God alone, not from the corrupt hierarchy of the church. It is probable that these female preachers and ministers had been fairly well educated.

Schwester Katrei (Sister Catherine) appears to have been a leader of a sect in one area. She proclaimed in a tract that through ecstasy she had become God. Her confessor is said to have replied, " 'Now leave all people, withdraw again into your state of oneness, for so you shall remain God.' " At the end of the trance she is supposed to have said: " 'I am made eternal in my eternal blessedness. Christ has made me his equal and I can never lose that condition.' " (Cohn, pp. 183–184.) Women at Schweidnitz (Lower Silesia) claimed that they had become more perfect than when they first emanated (a Neoplatonic view) from God, and more perfect than God intended them to be. Such arrogance, and such a level of education, would certainly not sit well with the male church hierarchy. These women gained large local followings, but it is difficult to know much detail of their movement, for church historians did not choose to record or transmit such information.

The Swabian "heretics" of 1270 said they had risen above

God and no longer needed God. Many Brethren of the Free Spirit became known as mystics, prophets, and performers of miracles. The church had lost its interest in miracles in its climb to power. The people still needed miracles and expressions of supernatural power, for that was religion to them, especially in the turmoil of the movement into the cities and of the plague.

The women in the movement of the Brethren of the Free Spirit tended to be of the middle and upper classes—women who did not hold jobs in farming or industry. Many of them appear to have been well educated. Cohn even suggests that the origins of the movement came from women, not from men, for it was the women who were totally deprived of any role in the church structure. (Cohn, p. 166.)

The early Beguines came from the urban areas of Belgium and the trading areas of the Rhine valley and Bavaria, and they formed their own communities, without vows, to perform charitable works. The living together eased the problems of providing for one's actual existence, for an unmarried or widowed middle-class woman in the thirteenth or fourteenth century might easily be nothing but a burden to herself, her family, and the society.

The Beguines were condemned in 1259 by a council of the See of Mainz. Monks and priests were ordered never to speak with Beguines or to go near their houses.

Here again arises the old fear and oppression of women which permeates the literature of the church. The woman who calmly gets married, runs the household, and raises children to obey their father is acceptable. Many women do not, or cannot, comply with this role. Those women who become sexual partners or marry for money and/or power are considered by the church to be degrading to men. Women who seek out roles that are contrary to those acceptable to the church-dominated

society and that provide women with power in their own right
—as preachers, prophetesses, community workers, and beggars
—are said to be run by the devil. Even the "virgin" fell into
disgrace if she tried to do more than remain chaste.

The Beguines also had the gall to translate the Bible into
the vernacular and to disseminate the translations to the people
—this, when only the wealthy could obtain enough education
to read. The pope condemned the practice of allowing non-
clerics to read the Bible. A Franciscan of Tournai accused
the Beguines of rejoicing in new and oversubtle ideas when
untrained in theology. An East German bishop "complained
that these women were idle, gossiping vagabonds who refused
obedience to men under the pretext that God was best served
in freedom." (Cohn, p. 167.) The misogynists could not tolerate
a woman theologian.

And so we again find women being accused of having the
traits of the oppressed—which coincide with the traits that
misogynists have decided all women have—while being forced
into situations where they could develop no other traits than
those of the oppressed. Women had little choice but to be
deceptive and cunning, or to be outright revolutionaries. The
Beguines exemplify the extropunitive traits of open aggression
and revolt, enhanced striving, and the strengthening of in-
group ties. The intropunitive women tended to accept their
position of subordination and to play their role in the man's
society, as did Etheria, the Virgin. They would strive for status
through making the right marriage and then competing with
other women for ascendancy in the drawing room.

Moving away from the heretical movements, we find at least
one woman, other than an abbess or a prioress, who gained
power and influence within the church of the pre-Reformation
period. This was Catherine Benincasa of Siena. Siena was the
home of much of the wealth of the church, and the home of

the early Renaissance which was in full blossom by the fourteenth century. Catherine, born in 1347, the daughter of a Sienese dyer, learned young the power of mystic visions. She became a member of the Dominican Third Order and served the sick and the poor. Then at the age of thirty-three she claimed that her visions commanded her to take public stands on political issues, and she went to Avignon to urge Pope Gregory XI to return to Rome. Later she served the pope as his ambassador to Florence, a unique event for a woman in the church.

In her letters Catherine always speaks of herself to clerics as "your poor unworthy little daughter Catherine," and then proceeds to tell the clerical personages of high rank exactly what she thinks of them and what they must do to serve God. For instance, she writes to Gregory XI:

> Therefore I beg you most gently on behalf of Christ crucified to be obedient to the will of God, for I know that you want and desire no other thing than to do His will, that this sharp rebuke fall not upon you: "Cursed be thou, for the time and the strength entrusted to thee thou hast not used." I believe, father, by the goodness of God, and also taking hope from your Holiness, that you will so act that this will not fall upon you. (Barry, Vol. I, p. 474.)

And to Pope Urban VI she wrote:

> Therefore I earnestly beg your Holiness to condescend to the infirmity of men, and provide a physician who shall know how to cure the infirmity better than he. And do not wait so long that death shall follow: for I tell you that if no other help is found, the infirmity will grow.
> Then recall to yourself the disaster that fell upon all Italy, because bad rulers were not guarded against, who governed in such wise that they were the cause of the

Church of God being despoiled. I know that you are aware of this: now let your Holiness see what is to be done. (Barry, Vol. I, p. 475.)

In a letter to an Italian cardinal she accused:

Oh, human blindness! Seest thou not, unfortunate man, that thou thinkest to love things firm and stable, joyous things, good and fair? and they are mutable, the sum of wretchedness, hideous, and without any goodness. . . . Oh, wretched man, the darkness of self-love does not let thee know this truth. For didst thou know it, thou wouldst choose any pain rather than guide thy life in this way. (Barry, Vol. I, p. 476.)

And to three cardinals:

Ah, foolish men, worthy of a thousand deaths! As blind, you do not see your own wrong, and have fallen into such confusion that you make of your own selves liars and idolaters. (Barry, Vol. I, p. 477.)

This last was written upon the involvement of the cardinals in supporting another man as pope when Catherine stated that Urban VI was the true pope.

Interestingly, Catherine had a large following when she was alive, with mystical sects developing wherever she went. After her death in 1380 a cult grew up around her memory.

Catherine served as a leader of the Tertiary, or Third Order, including men and women who frequently lived in separate communes while performing charitable works. The Tertiaries were connected to the Franciscans and the Dominicans. The order of Hospitalers of St. John of Jerusalem was the other major organization within the church where men and women helped the poor and sick.

By the end of the medieval period, as we have seen, the

church had become highly diversified, and the leaders, though striving to keep the church powerful, had become so much a part of the secular power structure that as economic and political developments occurred, the existing church felt threatened by the forces of change.

4. The Reformation and the Post-Reformation Period

The Reformation occurred during this period when nation-states were forming, cities were developing, and wealth was obtained through trade and piracy rather than by land ownership. The new rulers desperately needed money, which forced them into agreements with the persons in control of the money economy, the merchants. It was a time of insecurity and upheaval, with many "heretical" groups and movements, as we saw in section 3.

The Reformation itself did not liberate women any more than Jesus and the beginning of Christianity had liberated women. The reformers, still misogynists, even though their popular power and support may have originated with women, controlled the churches that had separated from Rome. Women, as noted before, appear to have been among the leaders in the formation of both Christianity and the Reformation, yet once the power hierarchy was established, women were left totally on the outside. Changes during the Reformation did, however, allow the ministers to marry.

The Protestant churches, by allowing fuller participation of the laity, provided women with a larger role in the church community. (This might be viewed as an expansion of the work of the Tertians.) The liturgy included congregational singing, psalm-reading, and prayers. Children had to be taught to read the Bible. "Women's Auxiliaries" would take care of the everyday needs of the church and the parishioners. The wife of the minister would serve as the "sister of charity."

With the development of the economy and early industrialization, the ideal grew in the Protestant churches that the man chosen by God, as exemplified by his profits and business success, would keep his wife at home to look after the house and to raise the children. Perhaps this was first of all an imitation of the nobility by the *nouveau riche*. With this ideal, though, developed the view that the woman must be protected from the evils of the world.

This concept of shielding the woman became the trademark of Victorianism. Women who had listened to unexpurgated Shakespeare in public places at the beginning of the eighteenth century blushed when they heard the same passages fifty years later. Whereas the women of the nobility had spoken the same tough language of the streets as did the poor in the seventeenth century, by the end of the eighteenth century only the prostitute would use such language. Though the ideal of the protected woman remaining at home received general acceptance, it was only an ideal and could be applied to very few families. The majority of women still worked on farms, in factories, or for middle- and upper-class families and men.

A sidelight of the official middle-class reform movement, dominated first by Luther, Calvin, Zwingli, and Cranmer, was the Anabaptist uprising in Münster in 1534. By force the Anabaptists deposed the civil and religious authorities. They claimed freedom from the pope and the local bishops, and proclaimed communal living as godly and Anabaptism as the one true faith.

Anabaptism included what today is called evangelical fervor, intense emotional experiences. The key question has always been whether the individual is possessed by God or by the devil. Sex undoubtedly played a major role in this fervor, as it did in the lives of all the mystics. This time, though, according to what records are available, the sex was acted out in physical intimacies similar to the "pagan" rites.

Well-to-do laywomen and ex-nuns formed a major part of the following of the Anabaptist leaders John Beukels and Bernt Knipperdollinck. (Cohn, pp. 282–283.) Many nuns had left their convents during the turmoil of the Reformation period and the early developments in industry. These Anabaptist women "began to see apocalyptic visions in the streets, and of such intensity that they would throw themselves on the ground, screaming, writhing and foaming at the mouth." (Cohn, p. 283.) At a peak of fervor the Anabaptists (led by the women?) took over the town hall of Münster from the Lutherans. The Roman bishop of the area responded by gathering mercenary forces to attack the town. Then the Anabaptists forced all the unbaptized out of the town—these being mainly the Lutheran middle class—and set up a totalitarian theocracy which commanded the sharing of all possessions. Many of the Lutheran men had left their wives and children behind. Executions and terrorism became the norm.

For a while the only sexual relationship permitted was between two married Anabaptists. But then, it appears, the ruler became concerned about controlling the women and increasing the number of Anabaptists. Because of the number of wives left behind by the Lutheran *émigrés,* and because of the number of men killed in the fighting, the ratio of women to men reached three to one. The answer: the preachers expounded the doctrine of polygamy. Beukels, the ruler, soon had a harem of fifteen wives. When women resisted men, they were punished and sometimes executed. Finally a law was established declaring that "all women under a certain age had to marry, whether they wanted to or not." (Cohn, pp. 293–294.) Once

married, the women had to fight and work to preserve the male
Anabaptist supremacy in Münster.

In 1535 the expelled prince-bishop regained control and in
1536 executed the Anabaptist leaders.

Thus the Anabaptist had performed the ultimate in the degradation of women and in encouraging the development of
the Traits Due to Victimization: hatred of self, of other
women, and of the oppressor.

As a response to the Reformation, the Roman Church held
the Council of Trent in the sixteenth century to clarify and
affirm what Rome considered true doctrine. At the Council a
new emphasis was made on raising Roman Catholic children.
Celibacy was reaffirmed. Marriage was raised to a religious
contract for the purpose of bearing children to serve the
Church of Rome. As marriage moved out of the realm of common law and into the realm of the church, so divorce became
nigh unto impossible by being considered the breaking of
what God had established. As a result, the ideal for the Roman
Catholic woman came very near to that of the new middle-
class Protestant woman: to look after the home, to bear children, and to give them religious training. But still the best way
for a Roman Catholic woman to serve God was to remain a
virgin. Both these patterns remained impossible for the majority of women who had to work and to marry in order to survive.

The Council of Trent also renewed the *Periculoso,* which
required all religious women to remain strictly cloistered. Bishops were urged to enforce the bull by the use of the police
power of the state, if necessary. Only the bishop could allow a
nun to leave the convent for any period of time, even in an
emergency such as a fire! Likewise, a person could visit a
convent only by permission of the bishop.

A few years after the Council of Trent, Pope Pius V issued

his constitution *Circa Pastoralis,* which required religious women to take vows of strict cloistering. Any woman who broke the vow was to be excommunicated, and only the pope could absolve her.

By 1572 the next pope, Gregory XIII, had to reiterate the cloister requirements in *Deo sacris.* In his constitution *Dubiis,* he required that any man, including the bishop, who had business in the convent must be accompanied by a group of *elderly* men and religious persons.

The women, especially those who had developed their vocation to the sick and to the poor in the towns and the cities, struggled against these orders from the all-male hierarchy. But eventually even the Ursulines, founded early in the century by Angela Merici, and the Sisters of the Visitation were forced into cloister and habit.

Soon after, Mary Ward and her "English Ladies" organized to teach and to work in the world, as an order parallel to the Jesuits. As was true of the Jesuits, they too intended to be subject only to the pope. The clergy objected, as they had for centuries, and in 1629 Pope Urban VIII issued a decree of suppression.

Mary Ward disregarded the decree and was arrested by three ecclesiastics from the Holy Office. Eventually the pope allowed her release, but issued a bull of suppression in 1631. The group continued as the "Institute of English Virgins," but not until the twentieth century were they allowed to recognize their founder.

For a woman, the alternative to the cloister or an economically secure marriage was to work in the cities or the mines, for wages lower than those of men. Even today women earn on the average only 59 percent of what men earn, within the *same* job class (Department of Labor, 1971). As a result, women were used as cheap labor, sometimes to defeat workingmen's organizations, which created deep hostility toward women workers. Women were also at the mercy of male foremen and bosses.

The noblewoman, having money and status from her family, could have the greatest amount of freedom and power. But even she could not hold political office except through her lineage, and thus had to manipulate those in office to gain her ends. The same was true of those women who married well.

As education opened up to the middle class and the laity, more women learned to read and write and became nurses and tutors to the wealthy. But the attitude of the churches toward women became embedded in the laws of the countries of Western Europe, and so misogyny won and the Traits Due to Victimization in woman became ever more deeply embedded.

There were, of course, exceptions to the pattern. Queen Elizabeth, for example, ruled one of the strongest and wealthiest countries in the world in the sixteenth century. Her independence and her refusal to allow the English Church to come under Roman rule so angered Pope Pius V that on February 25, 1570, he declared her excommunicated and deposed.

She has dared to eject bishops, rectors of churches and other Catholic priests from their churches and benefices and to bestow these and other ecclesiastical things upon heretics. And she has also presumed to decide legal cases within the Church. She has forbidden the prelates, clergy and people to acknowledge the Roman Church or to obey its orders and its canonical sanctions. She has forced most of them to assent to her wishes and laws, to abjure the authority and obedience of the Roman pontiff and to recognize her by oath as sole mistress in temporal and spiritual affairs; she has imposed pains and penalties on those who would not obey her commands and has exacted them from those who persevered in the unity of faith and the aforesaid obedience; she has cast Catholic bishops and rectors of churches into prison, where many of them, worn out with long weariness and sorrow, have miserably ended their span of life. . . .

Furthermore we declare her to be deprived of her pretended claim to the aforesaid kingdom and of all lordship, dignity and privilege whatsoever. (Colman J. Barry, *Readings in Church History*, Vol. II, pp. 71, 72; The Newman Press, 1965. Copyright © 1965 by The Missionary Society of Saint Paul the Apostle.)

But the pope could not prevail on Elizabeth, or on the people of England, and the Roman Church remained banned from England until 1829.

Roman Catholic priests who did remain in England had to be clandestine, and, according to many reports, were wholly dependent upon women hostesses to house, feed, and protect them. Yet a priest was taught never to be in the debt of a woman.

In the seventeenth century, Teresa of Jesus, the Carmelite nun of Ávila, developed an extensive following. She continued the tradition of the spiritualists' love of Jesus.

But when this most wealthy Spouse desires to enrich and comfort the Bride still more, He draws her so closely to Him that she is like one who swoons from excess of pleasure and joy and seems to be suspended in those Divine arms and drawn near to that sacred side and to those Divine breasts. Sustained by that Divine milk with which her Spouse continually nourishes her and growing in grace so that she may be enabled to receive His comforts, she can do nothing but rejoice. Awakening from that sleep and heavenly inebriation, she is like one amazed and stupefied. (Barry, Vol. II, p. 133.)

And in speaking to her sisters in the church, Teresa advised that the sister who wanted to achieve contemplation, to walk safely, must

be fully resolved to surrender her will to a confessor who
is himself a contemplative *and will understand her.* (Barry,
Vol. II, p. 137.)

Teresa went on to reflect upon the weakness of "our nature"
and the dangers involved in attempting to lead the contemplative life.

The reader cannot help wondering if contemplation was a
means of escape for Teresa from the position of women in the
world and in the church. She could not be a person in her
own right in either, and so perhaps she used spiritualism to
release the frustration and anger she held for being oppressed.

Vincent de Paul, in the mid-seventeenth century, held the
opposite view from Teresa with regard to the confessor and
the nun, or woman. In his talks to the Sisters of Charity, who
were poor village girls and daughters of workingmen and
workingwomen whom he organized into an urban community,
he advised:

> As soon as ever you feel an attachment for a confessor,
> leave him. He will destroy you (and you will destroy him).
> (Barry, Vol. II, p. 358.)

Vincent de Paul also warned the sisters of having a love of
money and of

> frequenting the society of men, taking pleasure in con-
> versing with them, especially ecclesiastics. (Barry, Vol. II,
> p. 358.)

He was much more realistic than the "saints" tended to be. But
here again we have the emphasis on virginity and on separation
between women and men. A modest woman never even looks a
man straight in the face, according to Vincent de Paul. The
sisters must love God, and *him* alone. The Roman Church

made Vincent de Paul a saint, but not the sisters who did the work.

The denial of human sexuality by the church had diverted open sexual expression to the realm of "the forbidden fruit," the hidden delight. The more it was suppressed, the more desirable it became. The more the misogynists labeled women as devious whores, the more women took on that role, and the more men wanted to have contact with such women.

The nineteenth century, that Victorian age of underground sex when the Vatican built up its library of pornography to be the largest in the world, brought the raising of Mary, the mother of Jesus, to new heights in the Roman Church. But these heights were based upon the belief that she had been freed from any taint of original sin, hence her Immaculate Conception, as well as upon the belief that she had borne Jesus while yet a virgin. Mary is said to be the mediatrix of all graces. And she is considered to be the second Eve (freed from the first Eve's original sin) and so co-redemptress with Jesus.

This worship of a woman in a completely male church may be an attempt to compensate for the unreal emphasis placed upon masculinity. Such compensation, however, cannot be viewed in terms of the needs of women, but must be viewed in terms of the needs of men, for Mary was thought to be especially efficacious in behalf of men and the church. By the nineteenth century, Christianity could again allow men to pray to a woman, a parallel to the "pagan" cults' worship of women. But, as Jesus was stripped of his sexuality, so Mary was stripped of hers, before the church would allow them to be worshiped, or at least to be the subject of prayers.

For men spirituals to speak of a sexual love for Jesus left them open to accusations of homosexuality, and the clerics were especially sensitive to this, for there was some truth in the accusations. And since the church had decided that homosexual relations were sinful and unnatural, it was even worse to be labeled a homosexual than to be accused of not keeping the vow of celibacy. In this context Mariology became a major part of the liturgy of the Roman Church.

The Protestants disliked the Roman practice of making saints, and accused the Romans of Mariolatry, worship of Mary. The Romans for centuries had defended themselves by saying they did not worship Mary or the saints, but only honored them. The Protestants generally did retain the emphasis on Mary's virginity, but otherwise did not try to make her superhuman.

We should note that it was in the situation where women were most thoroughly excluded that one woman was promoted to a position of having access to God. This woman was to be sensitive to all victims, compassionate, withdrawn, and passive (the intropunitive Traits Due to Victimization). Mariology did not catch on in the churches where women were able to participate, even though minimally.

Thérèse of Lisieux, France, wrote during the nineteenth century when this emphasis on the immaculateness of Mary developed and the extensive devotions to Mary appeared. Unlike her namesake in the seventeenth century—who was born into the nobility and who organized a new order of spiritual Carmelite nuns, and who was in fact a leader in the Catholic Reformation—the nineteenth-century Thérèse of France, also a Carmelite, was the daughter of a watchmaker. At the age of fifteen she followed her two sisters into the convent, and for the next nine years spent her time performing humble and trivial tasks. And so the name, the Little Flower of Jesus, for her simplistic goodness impressed all around her. In 1925 Pope Pius XI canonized Thérèse as the greatest saint of modern times. In her *Autobiography*, written under obedience to the mother superior, Thérèse wrote:

My God, you know that the only thing I've ever wanted is to love you. I have no ambition for any other glory except that. In my childhood, your love was there waiting for me. As I grew up, it grew with me. And now it is like a great chasm whose depths are past sounding. Love breeds love; and mine, Jesus, for you, keeps on thrusting out towards you, as if to fill up that chasm which your love has made—but it's no good. Mine is something less than a drop of dew lost in the ocean. Love you as you love me? The only way to do that is to come to you for the loan of your own love; I couldn't content myself with less. . . .

I'm certain of this—that if my conscience were burdened with all the sins it's possible to commit, I would still go and throw myself into our Lord's arms, my heart all broken up with contrition. I know what tenderness he has for any prodigal child of his that comes back to him. No, it's not just because God, in his undeserved mercy, has kept my soul clear of mortal sin, that I fly to him on the wings of confidence and of love. (Colman J. Barry, *Readings in Church History*, Vol. III, pp. 286, 287; The Newman Press, 1965. Copyright © 1965 by The Missionary Society of Saint Paul the Apostle.)

Especially with the nineteenth-century emphases on Mary, the role model for the religious woman had become the passive, loving, self-effacing, quiet, sweet virgin. These characteristics had been sought throughout the centuries of efforts to cloister the religious women. Thérèse, the Little Flower of Jesus, epitomized the desired role model and was appropriately recognized by Pius XI. Thérèse also exemplified the intropunitive Traits Due to Victimization.

Catherine of Siena and Teresa of Ávila were no such sweet, innocent "young things." They both tried to change the church and to lead it, and they both worked with men. Thérèse of Lisieux reached the pinnacle of the nonperson woman who would sit on a pedestal and not ask any more of a human relationship. She asked no more of Jesus, either, than to be able to love him like a father who would look after her and protect

her. The canonizing of Thérèse, the Little Flower, combined
with the proclamation of the Immaculate Conception, presents
a unified view of the nineteenth-century attitude toward
women in the Roman Catholic Church. This view of women
by the church seems finally to have toppled, officially, the individuality which women had expressed during the rural periods,
during the attempts to cloister nuns, and during the monarchies
when lineage was of real importance. Even as the churches
were losing political power they gained this victory in their
imposition of their view of women on the entire Western
world.

Pius XI made this attitude even clearer in his encyclical letter "On the Reconstruction of the Social Order" in the section
on "Support of the Worker and His Family."

> In the first place, the worker must be paid a wage suffi-
> cient to support him and his family. That the rest of the
> family should also contribute to the common support, ac-
> cording to the capacity of each, is certainly right, as can be
> observed especially in the families of farmers, but also in
> the families of many craftsmen and small shopkeepers. But
> to abuse the years of childhood and the limited strength of
> women is grossly wrong. Mothers, concentrating on house-
> hold duties, should work primarily in the home or in its
> immediate vicinity. It is an intolerable abuse, and to be
> abolished at all cost, for mothers on account of the father's
> low wage to be forced to engage in gainful occupations
> outside the home to the neglect of their proper cares and
> duties, especially the training of children. Every effort
> must therefore be made that fathers of families receive a
> wage large enough to meet the ordinary family needs ade-
> quately. But if this cannot always be done under existing
> circumstances, social justice demands that changes be in-
> troduced as soon as possible whereby such a wage will be
> assured to every adult working*man*. It will not be out of
> place here to render merited praise to all who with a wise
> and useful purpose have tried and tested various ways of

adjusting the pay for work to family burdens in such a way that, as those increase, the former may be raised and indeed, if the contingency arises, there may be enough to meet extraordinary needs. (*The Church and the Reconstruction of the Modern World: The Social Encyclicals of Pius XI*, ed., with an Introduction, by Terence P. McLaughlin, C.S.B. Doubleday & Company, Inc., 1957. Italics mine.)

Then Pius XII in his encyclical letter "On the Mystical Body of Christ" reminds Catholics that "those who exercise sacred power in this body [the Church] are its first and chief members" and that they must be maintained uncompromisingly. But those in the lowly places in the Christian community, including the mothers and fathers of families, can with God's help reach the peak of holiness.

The church as mother provides for all the needs of the members, or children. So through matrimony the church provides "for the external and properly regulated increase of Christian society, and what is of greater importance, for the correct religious education of the offspring."

Pius XII goes on to explain the superiority of the pope and the bishops, referring briefly to the virgins consecrated to God, apparently meaning nuns, not celibate men. The money of the church is to provide for the members of the hierarchy first. The people—the mothers, fathers, and children—come second.

John XXIII presented a fresh vision for the church, one that has since been clouded over. In his encyclical letter *Pacem in terris*, on the subject of the family, he wrote:

Human beings have the right to choose freely the state of life which they prefer, and therefore the right to establish a family, with equal rights and duties for man and woman, and also the right to follow a vocation to the priesthood or the religious life. (*Pacem in Terris*, Encyclical of Pope John XXIII, ¶15. Paulist Press, 1963.)

He too was trapped by the church's attitude into grouping women as wives, mothers, or nuns.

> Indissolubly linked with those rights is the right to working conditions in which physical health is not endangered, morals are safeguarded, and young people's normal development is not impaired. Women have the right to working conditions in accordance with their requirements and their duties as wives and mothers. (*Ibid.*, ¶19.)

No equivalent statement is made for men.

The Protestants in the post-Reformation period did little to improve the status of women in the churches. But many Protestant women did receive an education and develop careers in science, medicine, education, and writing. The Protestant milieu seems to have better prepared women for their own liberation than did the Catholic. Still the ideal of the mother and child persisted, even though the economics of the situation demanded the working mother and the working single woman. The secular governments of Western Europe recognized in the late nineteenth century this complete dichotomy between the "ideal" and the reality, and in several countries women began to take their places *next* to men in the work force—in jobs, in pay, and in social benefits. Child care was provided. And eventually as more men received the vote, so did the women. The United States, the one country in the Western world where a majority of the people are still members of Christian churches, though it gave the vote to women in 1920, still has not provided child care or a national health program, and only in 1963 witnessed the passage of the Equal Pay Act.

By the nineteenth century the image of women that was conveyed in the Pauline letters and in the writings of the church fathers had become a part of the Roman Church doctrine, and the intropunitive traits had been canonized as the model for all women who wished to overcome their "original sin." The

Protestant churches could not successfully deny the important role that women had played in their creation and continuation, but the more institutionalized they became, the more they excluded women. The High Church movement in England, for example, attempted to incorporate Mariology and celibacy into the Church of England.

Catholic women, then, tended to try to become Mary/saint-like in serving men, making no demands, bearing children for the church, and taking full responsibility for home and family, even if they did have to work. Protestant women were more likely to break away from this mold, to be able to obtain an education, and to make demands on and participate more fully in the society, the economy, and the political structure.

The Protestant churches, especially the evangelical groups, were in general more able to respond to the needs of the working classes and to the developments of trade unions. Questioning and change were not anathema to the Protestant churches as much as they were to the Roman Catholic Church. The more fluid situation in Protestantism was less oppressive, allowing women as well as men to play a role in the world around them.

5. Today

Many church leaders, Protestant and Catholic, have moved away from the image of women expressed in the nineteenth century, but the controversy over the status of women has not reached its peak in either group.

For the Roman Catholic hierarchy the main issues at present are birth control, abortion, and women priests. Before Vatican II, and in many dioceses even today, if the choice in childbirth is to save either the mother or the baby, the baby has to be saved. However, more and more Catholic women are practicing birth control and having abortions. Many women have reached the breaking point in trying to support a family without a limit on the number of children.

According to a June, 1972, Gallup poll, a majority (56 percent) of American Roman Catholics who were interviewed agreed with the statement, "The decision to have an abortion should be made solely by a woman and her physician." Yet the U.S. Catholic Conference in the spring of 1972 denounced the President's Commission on Population Growth recommendation for easing abortion prohibitions. In the same Gallup poll, 68 percent of the Catholics interviewed supported the idea of providing birth control services and information to teen-agers.

A few Catholic clergy have come out in support of allowing women to become priests. But as we noted in the introduction to Section I, only one seminary has accepted women students, and Pope Paul VI has no intention of allowing them to be ordained.

Several Protestant churches have supported efforts to allow medical abortions and sex education, and to distribute birth control information and devices. (It is worth noting that 64 percent of all the persons interviewed in the Gallup poll supported the statement quoted above on abortions and 75 percent the birth control statement.) These churches also have women in their decision-making bodies or have allowed women study groups or caucuses to appear before the decision-making bodies.

The Protestant churches also have women ministers, though rarely are women able to gain a pulpit or a congregation. Many marry a minister and/or become the director of religious education or the assistant pastor. The statistics are revealing:

United Church of Christ: 37 of the 242 women ministers (total of 9,000 ministers) have their own parishes.

United Methodist Church: approximately 300 of the 40,000 ministers are women.

United Presbyterian Church: 91 out of the 13,000 ministers are women; approximately 20 percent of these are full pastors. (*The New York Times,* August 3, 1971.)

With the present movement in the Protestant churches, it is conceivable that the number of women pastors will double even in the next year. The recent resolution of the Board of Trustees of Union Theological Seminary to set a goal of 50 percent women students should cause far-reaching changes within the churches.

Overall in the local parish today the roles of women remain clearly defined:

> members of the altar guild
> workers in the ladies auxiliary
> Sunday school teachers
> baby-sitters
> sponsors of teas, rummage sales, Christmas sales, and church suppers
> preparers of after-service coffee hours

The roles of men are similarly defined:

> ministers or priests
> readers (of the Lesson or Psalm)
> ushers
> sacristans
> altar servers
> trustees, elders, etc.
> officers of the church

Both men and women sing in most choirs and are organists.

The forces of change, however, are stirring faintly on the local level. In many Protestant bodies, women are being elected to serve on church boards.

The traditional concepts of the role of women in the

churches do not meet the needs of people. Some women have broken out of this role, but frequently at the expense of severe guilt, for their whole training, even in the public schools, teaches them that they are nonpersons if they are not married and do not have children. The churches are doing little to prevent or assuage this guilt. Rather, they tend to nourish it.

The women who remain in the churches, not rebelling against the role and position into which they have been placed, sometimes become vicious toward other women, condemning them for not suffering by having more children, for not being "subject" to their husbands. These women often support wars even though it is their own sons who will be maimed or killed. This level of desperation must come out of a severe self-hatred, the result of their own oppression.

Nuns seem to escape the vitriolic condemnations, rising above the whole issue by remaining virgins. But nuns today are running into conflict both with the clergy and with the laity by demanding some say in their own lives and in the life of the church of which they are a part. Although the church fathers praised the virginity of the nuns, they never wanted them near the wealth or the power. They viewed the nuns only by their sexual status. The present Roman Catholic hierarchy holds a similar attitude.

In April, 1970, 2,000 American Roman Catholic nuns founded the National Assembly of Women Religious and elected Sister E. Kennedy as chairperson. The intent of the Assembly is to gain "political clout" within the Roman Church and influence the position of the church on major issues. Many nuns are leaving the convent and are closing down schools in order to seek lives in which they participate more fully in the community. Sister Albertus Magnus McGrath (not liberated in name yet) drew applause at the 1970 convention when she stated:

Father says this is a clerical church; I say it's a male church. There is a presumption with regard to women that they're inferior, certainly intellectually inferior. Under Canon Law, women are not permitted to testify—nor are children or imbeciles. (*The New York Times*, April 20, 1970, p. 26.)

In May, 1972, the National Coalition of American Nuns declared they were putting "society on notice that women refuse to accept any longer the straw for bricks that we are forced to make." They demanded by 1976 full and equal status for women in churches, including ordination and proportional representation in church voting bodies. Further, and perhaps having the broadest implications, they called for broad-based research by organized religion into human sexuality, which should include homosexuality, alternate forms of marriage, abortion, and other questions affecting sexuality. (UPI, May 10, 1972.)

Yet during the summer of 1972, the all-male committee set up to advise Roman Catholic bishops in the United States on women's rights stated their opposition to the Equal Rights Amendment (proposed twenty-seventh amendment to the U.S. Constitution) because "it may very well destroy the unity essential to a stable family structure. . . . The impact on our social structure will be substantial." The Roman Church apparently fears desperately a change in women's self-perceptions and in their roles.

On September 7, 1970, the Vatican introduced a rite of consecration for young women "who vow to remain chaste while staying in secular society":

The votaries will be known as Christian virgins and will be expected to assist in missionary work according to their attitudes and abilities. . . .
The Sacred Congregation of Divine Worship which an-

nounced the plan, said in their statement that the new rite was "a mark of esteem for women, whose dignity is sometimes offended in our society, which is often dominated by vulgar hedonism." (*The New York Times*, September 8, 1970, p. 9.)

The Roman Catholic Church was accused in 1970 of buying Indian women to serve in European convents and of giving a profit to the priest in India who procured the women. The process appeared in the press as a scandal. For example, one Italian convent paid nearly $10,000 for twelve Keralan novices. But the procedure fits the attitude of the church toward nuns and toward women in general. Probably because of public opinion and of the higher standard of living, the church could not advertise in Western Europe for nuns, for money. In India the benefits appealed to the young women just as they did to women in Europe during the early period of the industrial revolution.

On the Protestant side, the Baptist women's caucus in 1970 distributed a pamphlet at the Baptist Convention pointing out the following:

Fifty-three men have served as president of the American Baptist Convention, but only four women. Statistics show that women do not have equal opportunity with men to serve on the church's major boards and committees.

Women pastors find few opportunities, and these are limited to small churches. Only 25% of local church Directors of Christian Education are women.

A woman Director of Christian Education usually receives less than a man would. The same is true of a woman pastor.

In January, 1969, only 29% of the women, as compared with 63% of the men, in professional and managerial positions were in advanced staff positions (department heads and above). In January, 1970, only 21% of the women were in advanced staff positions. (*The New York Times*, May 15, 1970, p. 7.)

The president of the American Baptist Convention and the moderator of The United Presbyterian Church U.S.A. in 1972 were women.

The Lutheran, Presbyterian, Methodist, United Church of Christ, and Episcopal women's caucuses have also drawn up demands and resolutions, most of which have been adopted by the churches. Here women are working together to gain equality for women. This is a trait due not to victimization but to liberation.

Such outspokenness and aggression are difficult for the men who consider the intropunitive Traits Due to Victimization the ideal to accept. The women who are fighting for equality undoubtedly have many of these traits, which are also the traits attributed to women by the misogynists, but they are trying to overcome these by organizing and approaching the power structures in an open, forthright, democratic manner. The power structures must respond fully and openly if the women are to be able to overcome successfully their ego defenses.

The churches today are not as powerful and not as sexist as they were in the past, but the legacy of past attitudes and actions remains the dominant factor in the attitudes toward and roles of women in the Western world today. When the churches excluded women, they left women to find their power and fulfillment outside the accepted institutions. When the churches viewed women as dangerous because of their sex and their evil power to pull men away from God, they made certain that some women would act out these roles (self-fulfilling prophecy) through sex and magic/witchcraft. Many women were thus directly and indirectly subverted into becoming witches, mistresses, and prostitutes.

The attitudes of the churches toward women produced in religious women mainly the intropunitive Traits Due to Victimization. But for many of those women who could not survive in this manner, the extropunitive Traits Due to Victimization became dominant. In several cases the churches exiled, tortured, or killed these women.

SECTION II

WITCHCRAFT:
A THREAT TO CHURCH
AND STATE SUPREMACY

WITCHCRAFT:
A THREAT TO CHURCH
AND STATE SUPREMACY

1. Introduction

Witchcraft, in the view of the Roman Church, involved the opposite of godliness, for witches gained supernatural power through the enemy of God, the devil. Witchcraft, therefore, became closely intertwined with heresy and the Inquisition. All three became predominant concerns of the church around 1300 and continued throughout the Reformation period. The consequent trials and executions had died down throughout Europe and the American colonies by 1700. But during those four centuries hundreds of thousands of persons, the majority of whom were women, were convicted of witchcraft and burned or hanged. (It is worth noting the definition of witch in *Webster's New Twentieth Century Dictionary*, Second Edition: "1. a woman supposed to have supernatural power by a compact with the devil or evil spirits; a sorceress: the term was formerly also applied to men. 2. an old and ugly ill-tempered woman; a hag; a crone. 3. a bewitching or charming young woman or girl. [Colloq.]"

At times the term seems to have been used to label any person whom the church or the priests disliked. At other times the term referred to a person who carried out specific rituals and liturgies aimed at producing an effect through supernatural powers. These rituals varied according to the time and place. But the trials of witches did produce a kind of hagiography for witches that became the traditional stories used to convict persons of witchcraft. These stories were developed out of the questioning and tortures conducted by the prosecutors, all men.

Considering the attitude of the church toward women which we examined in Section I, the condemnation and burning of women as witches was not illogical. As we saw, the church was not particularly tolerant of independent women and defined women by their sexuality, which was considered by nature sinful. The woman who was acceptable to the church was the repentant woman who spent her life cloistered or serving men in order to do penance for her original sin, the woman who bore the intropunitive Traits Due to Victimization.

As the church sought the source of evil in women, so some women used what the church considered evil as the means to gain status, power, and sometimes wealth. The church's belief in demonology gave women more opportunity for power than they would have had otherwise. These women unconsciously fulfilled the expectations of their oppressors and developed aggressive, extropunitive traits. But, if the records of the trials are a true expression of the feelings of the women accused of witchcraft, many of them had developed a self-hatred and a hatred of their own group, i.e., of other "witches" and women.

2. Historical Background of the Development of the Witch Craze of 1300–1700

Every early civilization had its seers, prophets, and oracles. Frequently these persons were ostracized by the existing power structure because their prophecies did not please the rulers.

These prophets appeared to the rulers to be undermining their power, and perhaps also to be leading the opposition toward open rebellion. The rulers would have their own prophets, who in turn would be opposed by the prophets who had not found wealth and favor under the existing structure. Constant tensions resulted.

The Old Testament is filled with stories of consultations between rulers and priests and prophets. Deborah appears to have been consulted and respected more as a prophetess than as what we know as a judge.

The oracles at Delphi, many of whom were women, gained exceptional power in Greece. They apparently had unerring accuracy in analyzing the existing situation, which suggests remarkable intelligence and insight. The Greek state had no room for women as rulers or voters or discoursers in the Academy. But untrained in sophistry and debate, and unconcerned with bureaucratic responsibilities, some women developed a perspective and a perceptiveness that was shown by none of the male rulers and that therefore allowed them to foresee the inevitable results of actions and decisions.

As societies became more wealthy and more powerful, less attention was paid to prophecies and to seers, except by the individual. The military leaders felt secure in their physical prowess, and women became more exclusively the means for their sexual satisfaction.

When the Holy Roman Empire in the West collapsed, the Roman Church moved into the power vacuum. The church hierarchy had no room for women. And, besides, the "pagans" had consulted women oracles.

The Christians, apparently when a minority within the Roman Empire, developed the theological concept of demonology. The Jewish tradition spoke of the fallen angels of God who lusted after the daughters of earth and took them as wives, but it did not have an ideology of good and evil based on God vs. the fallen angels. The book of Revelation gives us the first text for this struggle:

> Now war arose in heaven, Michael and his angels fighting against the dragon; and the dragon and his angels fought, but they were defeated and there was no longer any place for them in heaven. And the great dragon was thrown down, that ancient serpent, who is called the Devil and Satan, the deceiver of the whole world—he was thrown down to the earth, and his angels were thrown down with him. (Rev. 12:7–9.)

So the devil became the incarnation of all evil. And in the eyes of the Christians all the old gods and rituals and beliefs were evil. In actuality, as de Vaux develops so lucidly in *Ancient Israel,* the practices of Jews and Christians were very much a part of the world and the beliefs surrounding them. Just as the Jews set themselves apart in their return after the Babylonian captivity, so the minority of Christians in the Roman Empire set themselves up as the righteous select few.

> Consider the practice of Israel; are not those who eat the sacrifices partners in the altar? What do I imply then? That food offered to idols is anything, or that an idol is anything? No, I imply that what pagans sacrifice they offer to demons and not to God. I do not want you to be partners with demons. You cannot drink the cup of the Lord and the cup of demons. You cannot partake of the table of the Lord and the table of demons. (I Cor. 10:18–21.)

With Justin Martyr (second century A.D.) came the tie between the devil or demons and witchcraft, viewed together as evil and opposed to the godly. And because the godly hierarchy had to be all male, the means of the fallen angels, demons, to achieve their ends was expected to be via women, and, therefore, sexual relations:

> The angels had intercourse with women and begot on them children, who are what are vulgarly called demons; and these oppressed the rest of mankind with servitude, partly with magic, partly with fear and punishment, partly with the discipline of sacred odors burnt, and they scattered among men the seeds of all vices, lust, murder, war, and adultery. (Lea, Vol. I, p. 42; tr. from Magna Bibl. Patrum, I, 38–39.)

Early in Christian literature women were defined as the means by which the devil performed *his* tasks.

Clement of Alexandria (second century A.D.) referred to the fallen angels as those who sank into the pleasure of earth and revealed to women all their secrets. In this way women were to gain a supernatural power which was not available to men or to religious women through the good angels, who kept their secrets until the coming of the Lord. Men, however, could serve as the instruments of the good angels and God by becoming priests and monks. Religious women could become nuns.

Perhaps Clement is actually referring to the ability of women to prophesy and to serve as seers and oracles, an ability which the male Christian hierarchy could not tolerate, and so had to claim as coming from fallen male angels.

Tertullian, too, ascribed the existence of demons to the intercourse of angels with women. He claimed that it was the devil who perverted *men's* minds to heresy, always by means of magic and divination which was associated directly or indirectly with women and their sexual relations with demons.

But the height of the emphasis on demonology came with Augustine, who had been converted to Christianity from Manichaeism, which teaches that there are two *equal* forces, good

and evil, God and the devil. The Cathari, a medieval heretical
group, and many of the women tried for witchcraft claimed
belief in this duality. Augustine declared that women were
responsible for such beliefs because of their original sin epitomized by Eve, the source of sin because she was deceived
by the serpent which was the vehicle for the devil. The serpent
is also an ancient phallic symbol, so this view of Eve leads to
the belief that women are so lustful that they cannot resist the
serpent, or penis, i.e., the devil. (This is also the height of male
egoism—that a woman could not possibly refuse, or want to
refuse, a man's penis.)

And here we have the ingredients for the development of
witch-hunts:

Women are the tools of the devil.

The devil is the source of a woman's supernatural powers
(unless she bears the intropunitive traits).

Women will try to destroy men's souls, since men are
righteous and powerful in God, and the devil and
women struggle against them.

In this manner the male theologians identified with the devil
and demons the gods of the non-Christians and women who
had gained status and power through their abilities to foretell
the future. The misogynists had won, and in the church no
woman was to be trusted, for she might have the power of the
devil working in her. So to denounce women became the means
to protect oneself from the devil.

The writings of these centuries are full of stories of demons.
Two themes that occur frequently are the appearance of the
devil in the form of a beautiful woman and the appearance
of the devil in the form of churchmen who are found raping
women.

The former stories are connected mainly with hermits and
men living in monasteries. If a religious man so dreamed of a

woman, that woman had to be a demon. One particularly fascinating story is that of Gall founding a hermitage. When Gall sent his deacon, or guide, to catch fish,

> two demons appeared in the shape of naked women, and cast stones at him, reproaching him for bringing the holy man to eject them. He returned to Gall and reported, when Gall hastened to the spot and ordered them off. They obeyed, and afterwards through the mountains the demons were heard lamenting his advent. (Lea, Vol. I, p. 68; tr. from Walafrid Strabo, *Vita sancti Galli,* in Migne, *Patrologia Latina,* CXIV, 988.)

Later stories include the use of the sign of the cross to drive off Satan. In this way God was to become the victor in the struggle against the devil. The Manichaean conflict between good and evil had indeed endured.

As we saw in Section I, the thirteenth century witnessed the blossoming of trade throughout Europe. The Italian city-states became wealthy through their contacts and trade routes with the eastern Mediterranean. The Crusades had increased the wealth of the Papacy and the merchant aristocracy of Italy. The arts flourished as the patrons of the arts flourished. And the cities grew as the wealthy could employ more persons, all of whom needed services. Each state had to be defended, and the soldiers clothed, armed, and housed. The popes gained their share of wealth through war, trade, and tithes and benefices.

Even with this new wealth from trade, many of the older aristocrats were losing their land and their power. The money economy was superseding the bartering of earlier centuries. The landed nobles had no gold, only the produce of their peasants and what little they could collect in rents from the small farmers. Wars ravaged the lands of Western Europe. The soldiers had to live off the land and the people where they were fighting.

Rural life became increasingly insecure. Many women and men were forced to move to the cities and towns to try to find work for wages. The wealthy always had their mistresses. And prostitutes could earn enough money for food by being available to the soldiers when they were paid. When the soldiers were not paid, the women were forced to give their services for nothing or be maimed or killed.

As trade increased, so did the specialization of products. Cloth merchants set up systems of parceling out various stages of the work. In this manner those who had small plots of land could earn enough to survive. But when trade was interrupted, or the market glutted, they were left with no work and no income.

At such times people had to seek some means of survival. For them the Roman Church provided no hope, as it dressed itself in wealth and power. Other rituals seemed more efficacious. People did die when under a curse; the herbs did poison.

In this context of insecurity and of extreme wealth and extreme poverty, the church recognized a severe threat to itself through witchcraft, as people, especially women, exercised the powers of witchcraft and astrology to control their own lives and those of others.

By the end of the Middle Ages, as we saw in Section I, the church controlled all education, and men of the church wrote all the textbooks used in the schools and in tutoring, selected the sources to be read and studied, and determined who should be allowed to learn. As a result, all educated men knew of the association of original sin, Satan, and women, and had been trained to think in these terms.

The church also was striving to gain control of nation-states, and especially to dominate the rulers of Western Europe. In every district the local religious hierarchy struggled with the secular powers for dominance. As the church had become more powerful, so its goals became even broader, until popes fought with armies to subject all the people to the "truth" of God and of the church.

Heresy and witchcraft became keys to the church's concentration of power. Persons opposed to the church could be labeled heretics. Kings who refused to bow down to the pope could be deposed by the church. People who gave obedience to a deposed monarch could be excommunicated. People who opposed pope and emperor could be identified with different beliefs, and so be sought out to fall by the sword of God.

In 1233 Pope Gregory IX gave power to the Dominicans to establish the Inquisition. Inquisition courts were set up to function separately from the ecclesiastical and the secular courts, and they had only as much power as the local ruler or the local people allowed. But in the area of heresy, it was difficult for a prince to oppose the Inquisition, for such opposition raised the possibility of the prince being labeled a heretic. After all, anyone who disobeyed the church was a heretic. The Inquisition became especially powerful in Spain, Italy, southern Germany, and France.

Accusations of heresy were bound to become intertwined with accusations of witchcraft and sorcery. Theologians went through innumerable discussions trying to define heresy and the point at which witchcraft would be considered a heresy. In order to gain perspective on this, we might examine a few of the stated concerns of popes about sorcery and witchcraft, which also will give us a sense of how widespread practices and beliefs about magic were.

In February, 1318, John XXII ordered an inquest on several male members of his court accused of necromancy, geomancy, and other magic arts. In August, 1320, he extended to the Inquisitors the power to deal with persons who have relationships of any kind with demons.

A 1326 bull forbade

> all baptized Christians in virtue of holy obedience and under threat of anathema ever to teach or learn these perverse dogmas or, what is more execrable, ever to use them in any way. We proclaim excommunication *ipso facto* for those who disobey, and decree that those who do not correct themselves within eight days after the above admonition shall suffer the penalties of heresy, except confiscation. All writings used in these forbidden arts are to be surrendered for burning within eight days under pain of excommunication and other penalties. (Lea, Vol. I, p. 221; tr. from Raynald, ann. 1327, n. 44.)

But in 1330 the same pope acted to end the involvement of the Inquisition in Toulouse in sorcery trials.

Other references discuss popes' taking action against sorcerers at the request of royalty who think spells have been cast upon them. These illustrate the belief in the power of figurines and words. In 1336 Pope Benedict XII empowered the canon of Mirepoix

> to inquire and proceed against all persons defamed or denounced for heresy, schism, sorcery, or other crimes against the faith, with all the privileges of the Inquisition, in the Roman court or wherever the pope may be, and to invoke the aid of the secular arm. (Lea, Vol. I, p. 222; tr. from Hansen, *Quellen,* p. 8.)

Then in 1339 Benedict XII requested an investigation of some monks who had tried to find a hidden treasure by using a baptized image. Gregory XI in 1374 urged Inquisitors to prosecute and punish persons, including clerics, who invoked demons. Eugenius IV in 1437 broadened the role of the Inquisitors by ordering them to proceed against all Christians who "sacrifice to demons, adore them, seek and accept responses from them, pay homage to them, give written compacts."

The powers granted to the Inquisitors were broadened during the fifteenth century with an ever closer identification of heresy and sorcery, and with legitimization of existing superstitions and beliefs in witchcraft. By the beginning of the sixteenth century the popes referred to results of magic acts as true. But Adrian VI in his brief of 1523 tells of opposition by clerics and lay persons to Pope Julius II's efforts to extend his power through the Inquisitor of Cremona. Thus the popes in their support of Inquisitors eventually ran into opposition from the local priests and monks whose power was being threatened by the attempted authoritarian centralization. By 1578 serious doubts had been raised over the heresy of magic. Several theologians were attempting to distinguish between heretical and nonheretical divination and sorcery. Generally the heretical came to be defined as that which employs the sacraments to invoke demons or which renounces God and the sacraments. By this means the scholar could be a "humanist" and not be condemned as a heretic.

These distinctions appear to have developed during the High Renaissance with the general acceptance of classical texts, which included astrology and divination, as differentiated from theology. Intellectuals, including such persons as Marsilio Ficino and Benvenuto Cellini, and later Isaac Newton, believed in the reality of magic and necromancy and did not view these as heretical or as opposed to God. The church, on the other hand, had to exert its power and prove itself. Likewise, secular rulers sought to consolidate their power. Women and rebels were trapped: they did not have the defensive aura of scholarship or of any kind of acceptable power. The church and the rulers were bound to unite against them in the name of God so long as they could use women as the scapegoats.

So the church lashed out at the heretics and the sorcerers,

both of whom were unprotected by any existing power. The Waldenses and the Cathari were massacred wherever the local ruler also felt threatened by them. The witch burnings consumed people, mainly women, from the entire community, from the noble lady who was hated by the servants to the bourgeois town councilman's wife, to the merchant's wife, to the poor peasant girl, to the old grandmothers of the vicinity. There were many motivations to the witch craze, but the main responsibility must rest with the church and its attitudes toward women, united with its unwillingness to change and to share power. The turmoil of the times thrust people into insecurity, and instead of aiding the people, the church, through the Inquisition, added to the turmoil.

The church's attitude toward women made the persecution of women possible. And in witchcraft, too, women bore the traits of the oppressed: they turned on other women; they sought power and revenge; they did not respect themselves and so believed they were capable of all that the church accused them of.

Even when witches were tried in secular courts, the interpretation of the "crime" was based on the position of the church. Jurists accepted the existence of the devil, the sabbat, the pacts, the destruction of lives by baptizing figurines and sticking them with pins. Eventually jurists broke out of this context established by the church and took a different approach toward discovering the person who had committed a crime. But through the control of education, the church had been able to influence all the professions, including law, and the attitudes of all these men toward women.

Johann Weyer, the sixteenth-century Belgian physician, was the first person to question publicly the use of women's confessions under torture for things which no one had witnessed. As Weyer asks, Why should not the body which remains in bed *be* the very person who was said to have flown off to a sabbat and left a demon in bed? The search for evidence, for cause and effect, finally separated the law from the church in the area of witchcraft, but not before hundreds of thousands of persons had been destroyed.

3. The Malleus Maleficarum

The major church document that formed the framework for the persecution of witches was the *Malleus Maleficarum* (the hammer of witchcraft), published about 1486 and written by two Dominican theologians, Heinrich Krämer and Jacob Sprenger, who had been appointed by Pope Innocent VIII in 1484 as Inquisitors to wipe out witchcraft throughout northern Germany. The book went through fourteen editions between 1487 and 1520 and sixteen more editions between 1574 and 1669. The authors thoroughly believed the hagiology of witchcraft and presented this hagiology in the *Malleus* so that all Inquisitors might know what questions to ask and what accounts to obtain. Embedded in the questions and in the attitudes toward witches are the concepts of and attitudes toward women which we saw in Section I. For at least a century, apparently, all educated jurists took pride in basing their decisions on the *Malleus*.

The Inquisitors who prosecuted witches believed there was a conspiracy of wealthy, clever, well-led witches with cells in every district and sympathizers at every court, which intended to overthrow the prevailing order. Their means for overthrow, it was believed, extended from the use of curses and spells to kill rulers to the knowledge and use of herbs and poisons. Such is the context that the authors of the *Malleus Maleficarum* defined.

The two authors had become Dominicans while in their teens. Krämer became a Preacher-General and a Master of Sacred Theology in the Dominican Order; Sprenger, a Master of Theology and Prior and Regent of Studies of the Cologne Convent. Around 1474 Krämer, who grew up in Lower Alsace, was appointed an Inquisitor for the Tyrol, Salzburg, Bohemia, and Moravia. He became a close associate of the Archbishop of Salzburg. In 1480 Sprenger, born in Basel, was elected Dean of the Faculty of Theology at the University of Cologne and in 1481 was appointed Inquisitor Extraordinary for the provinces of Mainz, Trèves, and Cologne. In 1488 he was elected Provincial for the German Dominicans. In the 1490's Krämer lectured in Italy in support of the supremacy of the pope. Then in 1500 he became Nuncio and Inquisitor of Bohemia and Moravia, where he was to exterminate the Waldenses, the Picards, and the witch societies. Krämer died in Bohemia in 1505 and Sprenger in Strasburg in 1495. Of particular note is Sprenger's fame as the "Apostle of the Rosary," which emphasizes the role of the Virgin Mary.

Before looking at the *Malleus* itself, we can gain an overview of the situation through excerpts from the bull of Innocent VIII which gave Krämer and Sprenger their broad inquisitorial powers. (The full text of the bull is in the Appendix.) The Inquisitors received powers

> to proceed . . . against any persons of whatsoever rank and high estate, correcting, mulcting, imprisoning, punishing, as their crimes merit, those whom they have found guilty, the penalty being adapted to the offence. . . .
>
> [to] threaten all who endeavour to hinder or harass the Inquisitors, all who oppose them, all rebels, of whatsoever rank, estate, position, pre-eminence, dignity, or any condition they may be, or whatsoever privilege of exemption they may claim, with excommunication, suspension, interdict, and yet more terrible penalties, censures, and punish-

ment, as may seem good to him, and that without any right of appeal.

The *Malleus Maleficarum* is divided into three parts, each of which consists of a number of questions. The parts are:

The First Part, treating of the three necessary concomitants of witchcraft which are the Devil, a witch, and the permission of almighty God.

The Second Part, treating of the methods by which the works of witchcraft are wrought and directed, and how they may be successfully annulled and dissolved.

The Third Part, relating to the judicial proceedings in both the ecclesiastical and civil courts against witches and indeed all heretics.

The use of questions was the standard academic theological method of the time. The treatise is filled with Biblical and theological references.

The first part is of particular interest to us since in it the authors present their concept, in logical terms, of what witchcraft is and of who participates. Question VI lucidly conveys the attitude toward women: "Concerning Witches who copulate with Devils. Why is it that Women are chiefly addicted to Evil Superstitions?"

All wickedness is but little to the wickedness of a woman. Wherefore S. John Chrysostom says on the text, It is not good to marry (*S. Matthew* xix). . . . What else is woman but a foe to friendship, an unescapable punishment, a necessary evil, a natural temptation, a desirable calamity, a domestic danger, a delectable detriment, an evil of nature, painted with fair colours! Therefore if it be a sin to divorce her when she ought to be kept, it is indeed a necessary torture; for either we commit adultery by divorcing her, or we must endure daily strife. Cicero in his second book of *The Rhetorics* says: The many lusts of men lead them into one sin, but the one lust of women leads them into all sins; for the root of all woman's vices is avarice. And Seneca says in his *Tragedies:* A woman either loves or hates; there is no third grade. And the tears of a woman are a deception, for they may spring from true grief, or they may be a snare. When a woman thinks alone, she thinks evil. (Summers, tr., *Malleus,* p. 43.)

Krämer and Sprenger go on to speak of the virtuous woman, too, who brings her husband and her nation to Christianity. But the conclusion is that there are five reasons why women are more superstitious, and hence more subject to the devil, than are men:

1. Women are "more credulous."
2. Women are "more impressionable, and more ready to receive the influence of a disembodied spirit; . . . when they use this quality well they are very good, but when they use it ill they are very evil."
3. Women "have slippery tongues, and are unable to conceal from their fellow-women those things which by evil arts they know; and, since they are weak, they find an easy and secret manner of vindicating themselves by witchcraft."
4. Women are "feebler in both mind and body" than men.
5. Women are more carnal than men.

They conclude by stating that

all witchcraft comes from carnal lust, which is in women insatiable. . . . And blessed be the Highest Who has so far preserved the male sex from so great a crime: for since He was willing to be born and to suffer for us, therefore He has granted to men this privilege. (*Ibid.,* p. 47.)

Infidelity, ambition, and lust, then, are the three vices of women which make them especially susceptible to witchcraft.

These ambitious women who lust use seven methods to infect the venereal act and the conception of the womb:

> First, by inclining the minds of men to inordinate passion; second, by obstructing their generative force; third, by removing the members accommodated to that act; fourth, by changing men into beasts by their magic art; fifth, by destroying the generative force in women; sixth, by procuring abortion; seventh, by offering children to devils, besides other animals and fruits of the earth with which they work much harm. (*Ibid.*, p. 47.)

In this passage we find the heart of the male fear of rejection and castration which may be the basic fear that men have of women, especially of ambitious, aggressive women.

This emphasis upon sex and lust, as opposed to herbs and poisons, continues throughout the *Malleus*. When men are taught that sex is evil and that they can respond to women only in a sexual manner, they are bound to impose upon women their own neuroses. When sexual relationships are not part of the normal life, sexual drives must be subverted into other channels. The extensive worship of Mary by men who have taken vows of chastity is one example. The search for evil women is another. The preoccupation with women's "carnal lust" is a third. And when we come to reading some case histories, we shall see several other examples, including the searching and torturing of women's bodies.

Krämer and Sprenger tell one story that reveals the mixed emotions which are involved in their attitudes:

> We know of an old woman who, according to the common account of the brothers in that monastery even up to this day, in this manner not only bewitched three successive Abbots, but even killed them, and in the same way drove the fourth out of his mind. For she herself publicly confessed it, and does not fear to say: I did so and I do so,

and they are not able to keep from loving me because they have eaten so much of my dung—measuring off a certain length on her arm. I confess, moreover, that since we had no case to prosecute her or bring her to trial, she survives to this day. (*Ibid.*, p. 51.)

In the answer to Question VIII of the first part, "Whether Witches can Hebetate the Powers of Generation or Obstruct the Venereal Act," the authors suggest that the devil is responsible if a woman loathes her husband and so does not allow him to lie with her; likewise it is the devil in her that makes a husband reject his wife. Witches, and the devil, are held responsible for problems in the conception and bearing of children. (The midwife was frequently accused of witchcraft.)

Krämer and Sprenger go into detail about the kinds of pacts and acts the witches carry out at the behest of Satan:

They seduce young virgins.

They take young women to young men.

The witch lets the devil become her lover. She copulates with the devil, an act which cannot be seen by human eyes.

Witches teach young women how to bewitch their ex-lovers or the wives of same.

They devour children.

They raise hailstorms, tempests, and lightning.

They cause sterility in men and animals.

They transport themselves through the air, sometimes on broomsticks.

They cause themselves and others to keep silence under torture.

They affect judges and magistrates so they cannot hurt them.

They foresee the future.

They cause disease and famine.

They recognize the signs of death faster than a physician.

They participate in the black mass and desecrate the sacraments.

They take away the "male organ."

They change men into the shapes of beasts.

The authors seem divided about which is worse, the blasphemy of holy things or the sexual acts. But in the first part under Question XIV, they do say that the witches are worse than heretics, because they are apostates, since they give the devil

their bodies and souls. . . . They must not be punished like other Heretics with lifelong imprisonment, but must suffer the extreme penalty. . . . The penalty for them is the confiscation of their goods and decapitation. The laws also say much concerning those who by witchcraft provoke a woman to lust, or, conversely, cohabit with beasts. (*Ibid.*, p. 77.)

Yet all women are lustful, according to Krämer and Sprenger. And since no one can actually see the devil or his actions, cohabitation with beasts can be proved only by some person's visions or imagination. Where women are considered evil and dangerous, or a threat, visions of witchcraft and demons abound.

The headings in the second part, Question I, Chapter IV, emphasize the sexual evils of the women witches:

Here follows the Way whereby Witches copulate with those Devils known as Incubi.

How in Modern Times Witches perform the Carnal Act with Incubus Devils, and how they are Multiplied by this Means.

Whether the Relations of an Incubus Devil with a Witch are always accompanied by the Injection of Semen.

Whether the Incubus operates more at one Time than another: and similarly of the Place.

Whether Incubi and Succubi Commit this Act Visibly on the part of the Witch, or on the part of Bystanders.

That Incubus Devils do not Infest only those Women who have been Begotten by their Filthy Deeds or those who have been Offered to them by Midwives, but All Indifferently with Greater or Less Venereal Delectation. (*Ibid.*, pp. 109–114.)

In the third part the authors present in detail the steps to be taken by judges in order to rid the area of witches. They delineate the crimes which witches must be made to confess, by whatever means necessary. They set down the "truth" which the judges must obtain from the accused. They further warn that the witch must not be left alone, "for fear lest the devil will cause *her* to kill herself." (*Ibid.*, p. 226, italics mine.)

The judge should try to make the accused cry. But a witch will make herself look as if she is crying, when she is not. The judge must not allow himself to be touched by the witch. The hair should be shaved from the witch's body and her clothes should be removed:

For in order to preserve their power of silence they are in the habit of hiding some superstitious object in their clothes or in their hair, or even in the most secret parts of their bodies which must not be named. (*Ibid.*, p. 228.)

The judges must not consult

with sorceresses on behalf of the State; and this because of the great offence which is thereby caused to the Divine Majesty, when there are so many other means open to us which we may use either in their own proper form or in some equivalent form, so that the truth will be had from their own mouths and they can be consigned to the flames; or failing this, God will in the meantime provide some other death for the witch. (*Ibid.*, p. 230.)

With suggestions for the method of sentencing various "degrees" of witches, Krämer and Sprenger end their treatise on witchcraft. Their goal was not protection of the innocent, but conviction of the "guilty," no matter how many innocent perished in the process.

The goal was also to establish the superiority of God and the church. Anything that did not support that superiority and power by definition originated with heretics and demons. And since women had no place in the church hierarchy, whatever they did could be interpreted as coming from the devil. Here again we see the influence of the misogynists, through the church, in the witch-hunts and executions, and the further entrenchment of male hierarchies. From the *Malleus Maleficarum* the reader gains the conviction that the church intended to consolidate the central power of the pope vs. lesser powers even in the church, secular rulers, people of differing beliefs and nationalities, the bourgeoisie, the peasantry, and women. And the church leaders feared the power of women—which the church by its misogyny gave to women—more than the power of any other group.

4. "Evidence" Presented Against Persons Accused of Witchcraft

The title of this section cannot be the "Types of Persons Who Practiced Witchcraft," because all the evidence has been written by the judges and the accusers, and because a clear definition of what practices could be construed clearly as "witchcraft" is impossible.

During the centuries of turmoil and suffering, people sought their own means of power and security, and perhaps pleasure. The church and the Inquisitors lumped together everyone who did not accept or adopt the ways and the hierarchy of the church. In fact, however, there were several types of persons who were accused of witchcraft. In general they can be categorized as:

1. Persons knowledgeable about herbs and poisons.
2. Persons who made a pact with the devil for power, even if only in their imaginations.
3. Persons who arranged with other persons to bring about supernatural effects. These persons would also claim to attend the sabbat.
4. Midwives who used ointments at childbirth. Especially those who experienced a high rate of mortality of child and/or mother.
5. Old women.
6. Young, pretty women.

Persons knowledgeable about herbs and poisons. Doctors were not available to most people until the twentieth century, and even now the poor often have to depend upon "magical" or "wives' tales" medicines. The doctors of the past did not know much about the functioning of the body. The germ theory did not achieve acceptance until the late nineteenth century. Many times women would recognize illnesses and prescribe mixtures for healing which the official male doctors did not know. A number of cases called "witchcraft" consisted of women stating that a person who was ill would die within hours, when the person's male doctor was prescribing bleeding; or the women would prescribe a mixture that would heal the person, and the doctor knew the mixture as a poison. The woman would then become suspect for having a knowledge of life and death which only God and the devil were supposed to have. The witnesses, depending upon their response to the woman, would label her a saint or a witch. All healing seemed somewhat magical, at least to the intellectuals. And in the view of the latter, especially when they had adopted the misogynous views of the church, any woman who had knowledge or ability must be suspected of communicating the work of the devil.

It is probable that "witches" did aid in preparing poisons used to kill persons in revenge, or in plotting for power of various kinds. Poison was constantly dreaded by the members of the nobility and their courts, for in this time of instability the monarch was never sure of the throne or of the extent of the kingdom. "Witches" passed on the knowledge of poisons to their sisters and brothers and to their children, and in times of desperation, to strangers for money. This knowledge was a skill in high demand in the village community, and also in the urban areas. But the person who had the skill had to live in constant expectation of attempts of murder.

Persons who made a pact with the devil for power. Other persons were said to have made a pact with the devil. This pact had become part of the witch hagiology by the end of the fourteenth century. When a woman was involved in the pact—which was usually the case—it provided the woman with a companion and lover for life. That companion could show up at any time in any place in any form and demand anything from the woman. The two would have sexual relationships, and any children born of the union would be witches. The companion frequently appeared as a goat or a dog and would suck on the woman at the place which was thought to have the appearance of a smaller third breast, called the "witch's tit." At any rate, the woman who had a pact with the devil bore the devil's mark, and from that time was to be the means by which the devil brought evil into the world, just as the priest was to be the means by which God spoke to his "children." The judges always searched the accused for the witch's tit, or devil's mark, and would accept any spot on the body as serving the purpose. Psychologists have since discovered that psychological conditions can produce skin abrasions.

In the *Malleus,* Krämer and Sprenger refer to the conspiracy of witches, which had been mentioned by John Chrysostom. This conspiracy was supposed to have been an international organization through which the devil influenced people from the rulers down to the lowliest peasant or criminal. These witches were also accused of trying to overthrow the existing order administered by the church and the various nobles.

Person accused of conspiracy and of attending the sabbat. Other persons confessed to nocturnal meetings, sabbats, and meetings of witches at which they plotted their actions. God could not be mentioned at these meetings. The witches rode to the meetings on their companions or flew through the air—considered a magical feat until well into the nineteenth century. These witches generally were said also to have made pacts with the devil. But they always attended the meetings while leaving their bodies in their beds.

The devil was supposed to want to prevent childbirth, conception, and sometimes sexual intercourse, and to produce frigidity; and the witches were thought to conspire to achieve these ends. According to recent historians' examinations of the magic rituals conducted in rural areas, even when there was sexual intercourse, every attempt was made to prevent conception because the women did not want to become pregnant. The church did not approve of this. To prevent pregnancy, therefore, was an act of the devil.

Midwives. During an age of belief in magic, midwives assisting at birth, usually without training of any kind but needing a livelihood, were particularly vulnerable to accusations of witchcraft. From the cases on record it appears that the middle-class parents were the ones to bring accusations of witchcraft upon the death of a child or in the event of serious illness. And so it would be middle-class priests and judges who would be concerned about the lack of conception or about infant mortality. Women who did not want to become pregnant would not be so concerned with procreation as to accuse the incompetent midwife of witchcraft. And only women who viewed their role as that of mother would feel themselves threatened if they did not produce live, healthy children. The documents of the witchcraft trials give us a sense of the self-image of middle-class women who had become completely preoccupied with the production of children. Already the married woman without child was considered unloved by God, and perhaps under a curse. After all, since women are basically evil, the midwife could be drawing out the evil in the prospective mother. The accounts of the trials of the midwives never mention the filth and disease which were an integral part of all life at least until the nineteenth century.

Old women. Apparently women then as now had a longer life-span than men, and ugly old women, wise of the world, were objects of suspicion. Sometimes old women really do look like the proverbial "hags" and sometimes they do become senile. There were no face-liftings then, or false teeth. Also, various diseases can deform a person's features and cause the person to go insane. Epileptic fits and neuroses were not diagnosed as such until recently, not to mention the various kinds of severe mental illness. Families were not all they are made out to be by present-day moralists, and the accusation that the old mother or grandmother was a witch was not unusual. She could not support herself; she was probably ill, if not senile; and so she was an unbearable burden to her family. We still have no way of coping with old age within our society unless the person has an independent income. And we still see old persons wandering around muttering to themselves. Centuries ago those mutterings could easily have been imagined to be curses, and in some cases they probably were.

Young, pretty women. The young, pretty woman was also subject to accusations of witchcraft, probably because of jealousy and unfulfilled sexual desire. The man who looked upon a young woman with lust would accuse the woman of making him lust by means of witchcraft. If the woman did not respond to the man, this too could be cause for accusing her of witchcraft.

Since marriage was so important to the woman, she might actually try to use spells to attract a man. And if a woman lost a man to another woman, it is conceivable that she might try to cast a spell or have one cast on the other woman in order to destroy the new relationship.

The above types of situations in which mainly women were accused of witchcraft, as revealed in the records of the trials, do not clarify whether or not witchcraft was actually practiced, and, if so, in what manner and to what extent. I propose that witchcraft did exist in the minds of the Inquisitors and the church leaders; that at the time of the trials some persons, particularly women, practiced witchcraft; and that witchcraft did exist in the minds of the people of a particular area, including the accused, especially where the judges or the Inquisitors asked for mass confessions. We should therefore examine briefly the results of the psychological and sociological investigations which attempt to explain rationally the evidence given at witch trials and the acceptance of such evidence by judges for several hundred years.

The emphasis in the analyses made of the evidence presented by witnesses and by the accused themselves at witch trials is psychological. The pattern in the mass trials was the confession and the accusation of other persons made by the accused. As we noted in the *Malleus,* the judges and the legal systems of the time had no dictum of "innocent until proven guilty." Proof and evidence was sought to fit the preconceptions of the judges. The accusers found it relatively easy, especially through torture and questions, to gain the story and confession which they considered proof of witchcraft.

The confession and the answers to leading questions were accepted by the judges as evidence. Some who confessed also repented, but nevertheless the punishment was death. The repentant witch would be saved, i.e., could go to heaven rather than to hell. Psychologists suggest that the confession resulted from delusions of power, a wish for recognition and fame, and, in some cases, the wish for martyrdom or suicide. Actually most confessions were probably the result of the strain placed upon the individual by the accusations, the trials, and the torture. A person in a state of emotional shock can come to believe anything, especially in a society that emphasizes the guilt of the person for unknown sins. Women in particular would suffer from such guilt feelings in a church where they were told that they were naturally sinful and filled with lust, an easy subject for the devil.

To understand how much of a shock being accused of witchcraft must have been, we need to remember the conditions of the times. Religion was the language of society. The monarch held power from God. The merchant was successful because God was pleased with *him*. The woman bore a male child because God willed her to do so. The devil and witchcraft were powers of evil and therefore were considered to be at odds with the entire society. To be accused of witchcraft was to be deprived of any standing, honor, or respect in the community. Nevertheless, many women chose to take the chance involved in this course since they found it their only means of survival in a male-dominated world. But the women who accepted their role in society as inferior and subordinate servers of men were destroyed emotionally by an accusation of witchcraft. These very women would be likely to believe such accusations, too. Perhaps they had unknowingly succumbed to their evil nature.

All their struggles to be "good" became naught with the accusation and "proof" of witchcraft.

Other evidence used at the trials besides the confessions and accusations made by convicted witches consisted of the accusations made by persons who went into hysteric fits. These persons were considered to have been afflicted by witches, and so were asked who it was who caused them to suffer so. These hysterics may well have had no connection with any person at all, and if there was a connection, it was likely to be only in the mind of the hysteric. Other persons became hysterics under the questioning and tortures of the Inquisitors.

Hysteria has also produced markings on the body, including what have been labeled the wounds of Christ and, as we mentioned before, the witch's tit. The witch's tit would be the place on the body where the witch's familiar, or companion, sucked her blood, i.e., her soul. So long as the judges, or anyone, were looking for the witch's tit, they would find it, for no person's body is without marks, and hysterics develop unusual markings as well.

Once the witch-hunts began, hundreds of women became hysterical in fear of becoming witches. Dreams frequently increased the terror. When a person has a dream that ties in with a fear, the dream can seem to be real. The mentally ill cannot separate reality from unreality, and the people of earlier centuries tended to consider dreams real under any circumstances.

The good churchwoman probably had erotic dreams, partially as a result of suppressing her sexual desires. These dreams might include a man who would have to be interpreted as the devil. If the dream allowed intercourse, the woman would then believe she had allowed herself to be taken by the devil, and she probably would even believe she had made a pact.

Then as now, sexual freedom was quite allowable, and expected, in men but not in women. The woman who had sexual drives was a witch, was evil. The man who had sexual drives was normal. A woman could be trapped by a man who wanted to control her, for if she refused to have intercourse with him, he could threaten to accuse her of witchcraft; or if she consented, he could accuse her of acting at the direction of the devil by making him lust after her.

The judges used what today would be considered sexually sadistic means to gain evidence which the authors of the *Malleus* suggested was necessary. Besides looking for the mark of the devil, the witch's tit, they pricked the accused with long pins to find the numb place, which also could be the devil's mark.

The judges had women tortured, usually by burning them with hot irons or tearing their flesh, mainly from their breasts, with hot tongs. Other methods included the rack, the wheel, the thumbscrew, and tearing out the thumbnails. The women's sex organs provided special attraction for the male torturer. (Never in any manuscripts have I seen mention of a woman torturer or a woman devil.)

Women were also deprived of their clothing and all their hair (including body hair) during the trials. This action was taken, so the judges said, to prevent the women from hiding amulets or other objects used in witchcraft on their persons. And their vaginas had to be searched regularly "to see if they had hidden anything there." Men carried out these duties, too, there being no police matrons.

Men, as judges and clerics who could not get their hands on women any other way, must have found in witchcraft trials the means to their sick, erotic delight. And women did not unite and rebel, so well had they adopted the intropunitive Traits Due to Victimization—self-hate, withdrawal, in-group aggression.

The male judges had tremendous fears of castration. The

Malleus, for instance, speaks of women hiding men's penises in nests in trees. The *Malleus* also describes an example of a "witch" restoring a man's sexual powers by touching his penis. Of course, the devil had to be blamed for any sexual problems experienced by men, whether the problem was too much awareness of sex or frigidity. And so women used by the devil had to be responsible for arousing men or preventing them from having intercourse.

The psychology of collective behavior also affected many of the developments in the witch trials. People expected witches to exist. People feared sex and the devil. Men feared women. Men also lusted for women. Men feared castration. Women feared, yet wanted, sexual relations. When all these fears interacted, someone was bound to become the scapegoat for a mass hysteria. Once the church declared war on the devil and on witchcraft, every person had to feel some sense of guilt, so common were the practices of various rituals and superstitions which the church labeled "witchcraft." And we must not forget, the devil seemed to be at least as effective as God.

What today would be called mental illness formed the basis for much of the evidence accepted by the judges, and by the accused, at the witch trials. This is not to say that there was no witchcraft, for everyone believed in the devil, in superstitions, and in various rituals. The problems lay in the church's defining everything it disapproved of as coming from the devil, i.e., of being heresy or witchcraft, and then in accusing all persons involved in practices unacceptable to the church as witches. And since the church disapproved of women, women became ready subjects for witchcraft trials.

Besides the psychological and psychosomatic aspects of the procedures, we must also examine the medical evidence. The sixteenth-century Belgian physician Johann Weyer was the first person to gather evidence to refute the charges of witchcraft.

Besides looking for physical evidence of witchcraft, for some cause-and-effect relationship between the person accused as a witch and the person said to have been affected, Weyer looked for evidence of the sabbat. He found that a certain ointment when rubbed over the body caused the person to sleep and to have hallucinations of flying. So it is possible that "witches" used ointments to create effects such as flying which would convince themselves and then other people of the reality of their powers. Other ointments and herbs produced other effects, such as hallucinations, numbness, and long comas. The uneducated scientist or doctor would certainly border on witchcraft according to the concept of the church. Even Galileo had problems.

As the church lost power, the judges became less willing to carry out mass executions of witches. They began to follow Weyer in seeking physical evidence as the basis for conviction. Eventually the definition of witchcraft was narrowed, and the rituals were considered as parallel to the rituals of other religions.

5. Some Individual Cases

Prophecy

One case that did not end up in accusations of witchcraft, but that might well have, was that of Mother Shipton in sixteenth-century England. Mother Shipton's mother had been accused of being a witch, so a pall of suspicion hung over the daughter throughout her life. This woman prophesied first the future of individual persons and then of the nation. Because she was so often correct, she became highly sought after and well paid. So profitable was her business that her maid made a good living from bribes. Mother Shipton called Cardinal Wolsey a "Mitred Peacock." The cardinal, who received revenues from Lincoln, Tournai, Bath, Worcester, Hereford, St. Albans, Durham, Winchester, and York, was undoubtedly not the most popular person in the area. The cardinal threatened her with burning as punishment for her prophecies, but never attempted to carry out the threat, according to available accounts. Members of the church hierarchy, nevertheless, did not hesitate to consult Mother Shipton about the future. Prophecies could be most helpful in planning political allegiances, especially at a time when politics was becoming the name of the religious game in England. On the stone erected in Mother Shipton's memory is inscribed:

> Here lies she who never ly'd
> Whose skill so often has been try'd
> Her prophecies shall still survive,
> And ever keep her name alive.
>
> (*Glass*, p. 170.)

According to Justine Glass, this is "the only memorial in Britain which praises the memory of a witch." (Glass, p. 170.)

Mother Shipton, of middle-class status and social custom, fared better than her poorer sisters. For example, in 1616 a Scottish "witch," Jonka Dyneis, wife of a fisherman, was put to death for foreseeing that her husband was in danger.

A person who knows the future produces fear in persons who do not know, for the person who knows seems to have some special supernatural power. Again the question arises, Is the power of God or of the devil? In past centuries it had to be one or the other.

Perhaps then as now the political tenor of the times and of the community determines who is prosecuted and for what. If a person was not accepted by the community, any scapegoat tactic would be believed. Trouble usually is blamed on the ostracized. But once this procedure is begun, no one can escape. Any person who assumes leadership in a novel direction is likely to be branded. Between 1300 and 1700, the brand frequently turned out to be "witchcraft."

Joan of Arc is a particularly poignant example of this, and of the need for the use of religion as the language of acceptable action. Her experience reveals what happened to a woman who refused to play a traditional role and who refused to be used as a sex object.

When Joan, a peasant girl, had visions of the means to save France and make Charles, the Dauphin, king, she went to the local priest. At first he was suspicious of her, for the poor and those suffering from malnutrition frequently have visions. And, again, how was he to know whether the vision was from God or from the devil, especially since this was a young woman? Eventually she was taken to the Dauphin and examined by his theologians as to her faith. They finally decided that her prophecies were of God and gave her a man's uniform and a sword to lead the troops. In accounts of her feats, authors express surprise at her ready ability to ride, to wear armor, and to handle a sword.

Joan succeeded in having Charles crowned at Reims and in taking much of France back from the English. But when she was captured by a nobleman who was sympathetic to England, she was turned over to the English and no efforts were made by the new French king to assist her. The theologians of the University of Paris gave evidence against her. It would seem that the "savior" could not be tolerated once victory had been achieved. After all, Joan of Arc might not have been willing to return to shepherding the flocks. A woman with such powers as hers was highly dangerous.

The English proceeded to examine her. One English nobleman tried to rape her. The court told her that she could prove herself if she would wear women's clothing. (Who but a witch would dare to wear men's clothing?) But when she asked for her dress, the jailers would not give it to her. Eventually the theologians convicted Joan and had her burned.

Once she was dead, a trial of rehabilitation was held, and now Joan of Arc is known throughout the church as Saint Joan. Yet it is worth noting that the confession released by the Inquisitors and used as the grounds for burning Joan referred only to her usurping the powers of the male church hierarchy:

> I Jeanne, called the Pucelle, a miserable sinner, after I recognized the snare of error in which I was held; and now that I have, by God's grace, returned to our Mother Holy Church; in order that it may be apparent that not feignedly but with good heart and will I have returned to her; I do confess that I have grievously sinned, in falsely pretending that I have had revelations from God and his angels, Saint Catherine and Saint Margaret, etc.
> And all my words and deeds which are contrary to the Church, I do revoke; and I desire to live in unity with the Church, nevermore departing therefrom.
> In witness whereof my sign manual,
>   Signed Jhenne
> (W. S. Scott, tr., *The Trial of Joan of Arc,* p. 164.)

This confession is refuted by scholars as not having been written by Joan.

Pacts with the Devil, Sorcery

The witch trials on the European continent frequently included accusations of pacts with the devil and attendance at sabbats.

The Lancashire witch trials of 1612, which took place under

Protestant rule, gained fame throughout England for the seemingly extensive involvement of the accused with familiars. In the "forest" of Pendle in the early seventeenth century there lived two hostile families, both poor, one headed by Elizabeth Southerns, known as "Old Demdike," the other by Anne Chattox. Old Demdike was old, lame, and blind, and begged by the road for her living. Anne Chattox, an old, withered woman, worked as a wool carder. Both had professed supernatural powers and practices for years and claimed to have passed these on to their children.

When a member of the Nutter family, a wealthy family in Lancashire, tried to seduce Anne Chattox' married daughter and she repelled him, he threatened to evict the Chattoxes from the property on which they lived. According to the accusations of the witch trial, Anne Chattox retaliated by trying to kill Nutter by witchcraft. Other women supported her efforts because they wanted the land that the Nutter family held.

The feud between the families increased with charges and countercharges, all involving witchcraft. The justice of the peace had the women arrested. Then Elizabeth Device, wife of John Device and daughter of Old Demdike, who thought her husband had died from Chattox' curse, is said to have called a meeting of all the "witches" in the area at her home at Malking Tower to discuss how to release the arrested women.

Whether or not this meeting was actually held, the narratives of the trial claim that it was held and that it was an actual sabbat. Here, said the prosecutors, was proof that the accused women practiced witchcraft.

Old Demdike died in prison, but only after implicating all her enemies. The other persons who had been accused confessed to pacts with the devil, familiars and companions in the shapes of animals, and to the use of clay images. Yet there was no consistency in the stories. To add to the confusion, the judges and recorders of the trial did not speak with the same accent as the people of Pendle Forest.

Then Alizon Device, granddaughter of Old Demdike, became the chief state witness and went into great detail describing everything her mother and grandmother had done to bewitch people and animals, and how they had acted through animals, which must have been the devil. The accusations appear to have been part of a feud between two very poor families, for they charged each other with stealing, with laughing at a member of the family, with curses and bewitching, and with the use of clay images to hurt children.

The accused also admitted to suckling a familiar spirit, so the judges had their bodies searched. Alizon Device admitted to suckling a dog; Elizabeth, to having been sucked for forty years at a place on her left side.

In most trial accounts, the main theme of the confessions of pacts made with the devil is that when a woman consented to give the devil her soul, she was promised "that from thenceforward she would want for nothing and be avenged on whom she would." (Peel, p. 30.)

The king of England at the time, James I, considered himself a target for the devil. He even attended witch trials, though not the one described above, and was particularly eager for the execution of witches. In 1597, before he had become king, he had published his own study of witchcraft, *Demonology*. And in this book he stated:

> I call them witches which do renounce God and yield themselves wholly to the Devil. . . .
> Usually, the familiar shows unto them [the witches] in the likeness of a dog, a cat, an ape, or such like beasts. (Peel, p. 34.)

James I also supported the use of the prick to find a numb spot on a witch's body which could be the devil's mark. And the most likely place to find the devil's mark, he said, was on the breasts or around the vagina.

It is no wonder, then, that in the country under this king's rule Old Demdike, Anne Chattox, members of their families, and their associates were hanged as witches. One woman, Alice Nutter, of the local wealthy family, appears to have been accused purely out of spite, and she was hanged on the basis of testimony given by the great-granddaughter of Old Demdike, nine-year-old Jennet Device. Jennet managed to have her entire family hanged, except for her brother, James.

Clerical "Witchcraft"

Many clergy appear to have had a particular fascination with witchcraft. For example, Giraldus Cambrensis reported in the twelfth century that some priests celebrated Mass over wax images in order to curse someone. Joseph Hansen reports in his works on witchcraft and sorcery numerous cases of clergy coming before the ecclesiastical courts on charges of practicing witchcraft.

One of the latter cases, which came before the archepiscopal court of Toulouse in 1323, found the prior of St.-Sulpice guilty of using leaden images to discover hidden treasure. He failed to find the treasure and explained the failure as due to the fact that he had not made the images under the right constellation.

In other cases sex appears to have been a major part of what was considered witchcraft among the clergy. For example, in 1282 the priest of Inverkeiting was accused of leading a fertility dance in the churchyard.

Jules Michelet reports in detail a case of sex, witchcraft, and religion in the Ursuline convent in Provence in 1610. The priest Gauffridi, already known as "lover-general of the nuns" in the

Convent of le Quesnoy, arrived at the Ursuline convent. (At this time in Paris, women who had had sexual relations with priests were called "the sanctified.") Two women in the convent, Madeleine and Louise, claimed Gauffridi as their lover. Concerned for his own well-being, Gauffridi took them to the local Inquisitor to have their evil spirits exorcised. Madeleine, Michelet reports, was physically examined with no matron present by the Inquisitor and the judges, who presumably were looking for the devil's mark. After this experience Madeleine delighted in describing at great length her love for and dreams of Gauffridi and her trips to the sabbat where the magicians adored her body.

Another Inquisitor decided to arrest Gauffridi and charge him with witchcraft. He was pricked and found insensitive in three places. He then confessed all that he had actually done, in order to save his life by proving his infamy and his innocence of witchcraft. The Capuchin monks, however, while sheltering Gauffridi and giving him sympathy, convinced him that he should confess to witchcraft. The two women were not executed; Gauffridi was. The women were made to prostrate themselves before the judges, and after the trial, Madeleine was kept by the priests to cut wood to be sold for charitable purposes. Louise went free and proceeded to denounce persons and to accuse them of magic and sorcery, an effective revenge.

Michelet also reports a case of the eighteenth century involving the Jesuits and the Observantine Fathers and their relationships with women, both in and out of the convents. Some of the priests lived with their mistresses. They

lived in open concubinage with their penitents; nay: they were not satisfied with this iniquity, but even failed to respect the little girls who were pupils at the nunnery. The Father Superintendent (Observantine), one Aubany, had violated one, a child of thirteen, afterwards flying to Marseilles to escape the vengeance of her relatives. (Michelet, p. 232.)

Father Girard, a Jesuit living in eighteenth-century France, had developed with Madam Guiol, daughter of a cabinetmaker, a relationship which gave him access to middle-class women who came to the parlor of the Ursuline nuns to be taught. Witchcraft enters into this eighteenth-century situation only as the penitent Charlotte Cadière began to believe herself possessed by the devil because of the seeming hypocrisy of her sexual and religious involvement with the priest, Father Girard.

In 1730 Father Girard had Charlotte brought to trial as a means to protect himself. A conflict between Jesuits and Jansenists resulted, with the Jansenists being sympathetic to Charlotte. Charlotte admitted to divining the secrets of other persons, mainly women, and so was accused of witchcraft. Girard, on the other hand, was considered to have been the "plaything, the victim of enchantment." (Michelet, p. 302.) The parlement (French court) sentenced Charlotte to death. The Jansenists tried to stop the execution and appear to have succeeded, though at this juncture Charlotte disappeared. Girard died peacefully in 1733, a Jesuit in good standing.

Hysteria

The best examples of hysterics come from accounts of the New England witch trials. The entire history of the Salem witch craze, for example, is riddled with persons having fits, whether the person was the accused or the supposed victim.

In Hartford, Connecticut, in 1662, Anne Cole went into fits in church and during prayers cried out in strange voices. The voices claimed that she and several other persons had familiarity with the devil. Anne did not remember any of this when she came out of the fit, but she did confess to being a witch and " 'that the Devil had frequent use of her body with much seeming (but indeed horrible, hellish) delight to her.' " (Chadwick Hansen, *Salem*, p. 37.)

In 1688 in Boston, Cotton Mather began the examination of Sarah Good, an old woman from Salem who was accused by children of afflicting them with hysteria, pain, and convulsions. No one could see the specter of witches other than the children. Sarah Good appears to have become the scapegoat of the town, for her neighbors blamed a number of unexplainable events on her and stated that her mutterings were really curses. Sarah Good was eventually condemned and executed. When Rev. Nicholas Noyes called upon her to confess on the gallows, she replied:

> "You are a liar. . . . I am no more a witch than you are a wizard, and if you take away my life God will give you blood to drink." (Chadwick Hansen, *Salem*, p. 167, in George Lincoln Burr, *Narratives of the Witchcraft Cases, 1648–1706*, p. 358; 1914, repr. 1959, Barnes & Noble.)

Rebecca Nurse was accused of being a witch, but when thirty-nine of her neighbors signed a petition declaring her innocence, the jury found her not guilty. The accusers, hysterics, were so upset that they cried out in court. The judges then reconsidered the case. Rebecca Nurse's relatives brought a stronger case in her behalf, and the judge granted her a reprieve. Immediately the accusers cried out that they were being tormented again. The reprieve was withdrawn. The church in Salem Town excommunicated Rebecca Nurse, stating that she was a convicted witch. She was hanged.

Abigail Hobbes was a rebellious child and adult, and so gained the reputation of being a witch—she even claimed to be a witch. She disobeyed her father, mother, and church, and

she claimed she was not afraid of anything. Finally she announced that she had made a bargain with the devil, which
gave her ultimate power over everyone. She was officially tried
as a witch and condemned to death, though the execution was
stayed when she "confessed" a second time.

Rural Witchcraft

A somewhat different situation existed with regard to rural
witchcraft, where the emphasis was on forces of nature. For
example, in 1510 sixty men and women were burned at Val-
Camonica near Brescia, Italy, for causing men and women and
animals to be sick and for destroying harvests. (Lea, Vol. I, p.
242.) The following year nearly sixty women confessed under
torture to attending the sabbat.

In 1466, according to Joseph Hansen, Hans Heyman confessed under torture to causing avalanches with the help of
several witches, and to causing snow and frost. (Lea, Vol. I,
p. 249.) In 1450, in Lucerne, Else von Meersburg confessed to
having caused hailstorms for many years. In France in the
1450's, several persons confessed to causing unseasonably cold
spring weather which destroyed the vegetation.

In the late fifteenth century in the Cévennes, many village
women were accused of celebrating the religion of the goat-
devil,

> with its customary rites of kissing his ass, frigid embraces,
> dances, offerings of black candles, trampling upon the
> cross, and insults to the Virgin (nicknamed the Redhead,
> *la Rousse*). (Monter, p. 165; tr. from Ladurie.)

One of the women, Martiale, was accused of poisoning children, stealing wine, and casting spells. The Huguenots eventually converted the people in this area to Christianity.

Farther north in the Vivarais mountains, Louise Fumat "was hanged for having trampled on the cross, prostituted her body, killed her husband and having attended the Sabat." (Monter, p. 166; tr. from Ladurie.) Her judge confiscated her property. Between 1519 and 1530, other women in the area were burned for bewitching newlyweds and pigs, spitting upon the Host, and dancing around a goat.

The case of Thomas Platter in 1596 exposes a psychotic fear of castration, then known as ligature. Women witches were considered responsible. In Languedoc the fear reached such proportions that couples did not marry publicly.

Mistress and "Witch"

One final example of witchcraft is the case of Madame de Montespan, mistress of King Louis XIV. Fearing that the king was losing his affection for her, Mme. de Montespan felt that she needed to do something to protect her position. She went to La Voisin, the infamous Frenchwoman of high birth who knew and used the arts of potions, herbs, poisons, and spells. The more upset Mme. de Montespan became, the more drastic the measure that she felt compelled to try. According to reports of her trial testimony, she fed to the king bat's blood, desiccated mole, and cantharides. (Cantharides is "a preparation of Spanish flies, used internally as a diuretic or genitourinary stimulant, and externally as a skin irritant." *Webster's New Twentieth Century Dictionary*.) According to popular accounts of Mme. de Montespan's testimony, which was given under torture, in 1672 the Abbé Guibourg performed an amatory mass using Mme. de Montespan's naked body as the altar. By 1679 she had lost all hope of regaining the king's affection and so had a mortuary mass performed, and when that failed to kill the king, she planned to poison him. La Voisin was burned in 1680 for her treacherous acts. When Mme. de Montespan came under suspicion, the king protected her, pensioned her off to the country, and burned her testimony.

6. Today

In the above cases we see exemplified the many different motivations of both the accusers and the accused. But we see also the seriousness with which people considered witchcraft and demonology.

The basis for all religion is the conviction of persons that there are supernatural powers. Beliefs and rituals have developed around concepts of the means to appease and to control the supernatural. The Greeks had their means, the Romans theirs. Then the Christians set up different belief structures and rituals, and they called all persons who did not agree with them pagans or heretics. Originally this was probably a defense mechanism, since the Christians were so small an elite, and so persecuted. As they gained power and influence, they viewed persons of other beliefs as being as much of a threat as the Romans had originally viewed them, the Christians.

Because the Christians, with their misogynous attitudes, had become so powerful by the end of the thirteenth century, and because the church sought to increase its power through the turmoil of the times, persons oppressed by the church were bound to rebel. And through the development of the theology of demonology in the preceding centuries, the Inquisitors obtained the rationale for the persecution of those who rebelled, accusations of witchcraft. Perhaps the most amazing aspect of the history of the witchcraft trials is the length of time that people, especially women, put up with this arbitrary use of power. Eventually people organized to take political and economic action that would establish limits to this power, but the women still were not free from oppression.

By the eighteenth century, the church had declined in political and economic power. The nation-state had become the dominant organization which collected the taxes and governed people's lives. The church no longer had the influence to conduct witchcraft trials. The state used such trials only in the political arena, to rid itself of its enemies. And the church itself was curtailed by the state. In some areas the clergy were hunted like witches who were trying to use the supernatural to overthrow the government.

The hagiography of witches disappeared, but misogyny and the rituals of witchcraft continued. Misogynists now played the roles of middle-class merchants, intellectuals, and politicians who kept their women at home and "provided" for them and "protected" them. These same men had their mistresses who were to satisfy their sexual needs and boost their egos. The clerics did not stop oppressing women, but their positions of power and direct influence had been partially usurped.

Women continued to bear the characteristics of the oppressed and to gain power and influence by means which the male order considered subversive. In the eighteenth century in the urban areas, the methods became more sexual than magical, but the motivations remained the same. In Section III we shall look in detail at the sexual roles of women in male-dominated societies. But first we need to take a look at the place of witchcraft in the twentieth century.

By the middle of the twentieth century, many persons in the urban middle class were turning to astrology, extrasensory perception, fortune-telling, tarot cards, and witchcraft. Attendance at churches dropped. People questioned the relevancy and meaning of the Mass and liturgies. No power resulted from such practices, they thought, and no sense of

reality was conveyed. The two world wars, the highly cen-
tralized bureaucratic governments, the political parties which
had no room for the people and their concerns, left a sense of
powerlessness over one's own destiny. Rituals of rebellion
sprang up throughout the world. The Mau Mau held ritual
murders, as did motorcycle gangs. Persons began taking drugs
to allow themselves "freedom of action."

In the United States, the military might of the government
grew beyond all conception of possibilities of control, and the
means to power and influence outside the "system" became
guerrilla tactics, bombings, stabbings, curses, and the rituals
of witchcraft. Women have frequently organized and led these
"antisocial" actions. The government has reacted in panic to
an irrational fear of the power of rebellion and has begun
using force tactics and various forms of torture and harass-
ment.

Women do not play the major role among the objects of the
present repression. They have been submerged for too many
centuries to appear to threaten the power structure. The faith
today is in military might, and women have no access to this.
But if the belief in magic, astrology, and witchcraft grows, and
the misogynists' attitudes toward women are embedded in the
belief, then women will again become the objects of the witch
trials.

Actually, advocates of women's rights are today attacked in
some places as the witches of modern times. One feminist
leader reports how the members of the women's group of a
suburban church responded with almost psychopathic anger
and hatred to a modest address on the women's movement.

The women who become liberated seek open means to an
equal share in the power, as did the political parties and the
labor unions of the late nineteenth century. But the women
who remain oppressed continue to use devious ways to influ-

ence, control, or hurt other people, both men and women. These women today generally do not use the methods of traditional witchcraft, but they do make deals for power, and they do fulfill the characteristics of the women whom the misogynists portray as lustful, out to take a man's sexual powers, to use him for their own ends.

SECTION III

SEX:

THE SELF-DESTRUCTIVE WEAPON

SECTION III

SEX:
THE SELF-DESTRUCTIVE WEAPON

1. Introduction

Religion and magic do not determine sex roles any more than sex determines magic and religion. Nevertheless, the three are closely intertwined.

As mentioned in Section I, the early Christians needed to set themselves off from "pagans," and the most obvious way to do this was to deny the pleasure of sexual relationships. The concern about sex made attitudes toward sex, and hence toward women—by the all-male church—an important part of the church doctrine, structure, liturgy, and function.

The belief in magic and the devil was also bound to be associated with sex in the view of the church. Since sex was evil, sex was of the devil. Since women brought on sexual stimulation, women were of the devil. The witch trials gave churchmen a wonderful opportunity to look at women's nude bodies, to touch them, to examine them in every detail, and to torture them. And women had to be subjected to this because it was the law, and the law was God.

But as we saw in Section II, magic and witchcraft were one means used by women to attain power. This means, though, would never have been so successful without the church's belief in the devil, its preoccupation with sex, and its misogynous attitude toward women. The other main means to wealth or power available to women, sex, likewise depended upon the church for its success. The definition of women, but *not* of men, by their sexual function both forced women into sexual roles, whether by choice or not, and guaranteed that men, especially churchmen, would think of nothing but sex every time they saw a woman.

The above seems to be a gross generalization. Two years ago it would not even have occurred to me. In the last few months, though, I have consciously discussed this with men of all levels of education, varying professions, different economic classes, and all races, and every man, except two or three, either admitted that his vantage of women is first sexual and then *perhaps* professional, or stated that women dress the way they do so he will look at them only sexually. Many of the men feared for their own sexuality, commenting they would worry when they stopped "looking" at women.

Madison Avenue has picked up this emphasis in advertising. Advertisers depend upon the sex appeal of women to sell products to men, and upon the mother image to sell products to women. For the former, if the advertisement can convince women that if they use a product, they will be more appealing to men, then the sex appeal can be used on women too. During the 1960's the women who "made it" in the films were the dumb-blond, large-breasted, swinging-hips types, some of whom may have been very intelligent and even good actresses, given the chance. One of the biggest sensations in New York City in recent years occurred when the men of Wall Street jammed the streets to gain a glimpse of a woman with enormous breasts.

This voyeur aspect of sex may well be closely tied to the mother image of women, via the oedipal theories and the church's sanction of woman as mother. Woman must be mother. And mother to the tiny baby is synonymous with breast, warmth, and nourishment, i.e., oral satisfaction. Perhaps men still want the mother image, though they disguise this by responding to the sex appeal.

The church has historically related sex and motherhood by labeling the former as evil, the latter as good. No wonder the pope is concerned about the talk of birth control and abortions. Perhaps if women do not have several children to look after, they will have time to seduce men, and to make their way into the hierarchy of the church. For women to be free of the sex object and motherhood stereotyping would be for them to be free to function as persons in the society.

2. Prostitution

Webster's New Twentieth Century Dictionary defines "prostitute":

verb: 1. to sell the services of (oneself or another) for purposes of sexual intercourse;
2. to sell (oneself, one's artistic or moral integrity, etc.) for low or unworthy purposes.

adj.: debased; corrupt; sold to wickedness or to base purposes.

noun: 1. a *woman* who engages in *promiscuous* sexual intercourse for pay; whore; harlot;
2. a person, as a writer, artist, etc., who sells *his* services for low or unworthy purposes. (Italics mine.)

The definition itself conveys that the "promiscuity," the sin-evil-devil, rests with the woman who prostitutes herself, who is the prostitute, because it is *she* who is to receive the money, *she* who lures the man, *she* who is not an "upright" citizen.

The dictionary does not reveal the many facets of prostitution, nor does it convey the full meaning of the profession in terms of the individuals involved or the social-economic-political context. It does not mention, for example, that all the male clients are called "Johns," or that the sexual act is referred to as "turning a trick."

A psychiatrist once compared the woman giving her body in an attempt to gain a friend to the adult giving candy to the child in order to gain affection and trust. Both of these situations are established by the assumptions of the society as to the nature of the people involved. In the former, women assume that men want only sex and, with luck, friendship may follow. In the latter, the adult assumes that the child will do anything if given candy. The reverse, of course, also occurs, especially in a society where the assumptions exist that the only possible relationship between women and men is sexual, and between adult and child is the giving and receiving of goods.

Yet both attempts fail. The woman does not gain a friend, and the child learns to manipulate the adult. That a woman is seeking friendship does not even occur to most men, for according to the mass media and Madison Avenue, all *women* want is sex. Here are the misogynous attitudes again, and here again are women adopting the characteristics attributed to them in an attempt to gain what they may really want: love, a friend.

Jack Dominian, staff psychiatrist to the Catholic Marriage Guidance Council in England, printed a fictional letter in the pamphlet *Getting Married*, published by the British Medical Association, in which the husband reproaches his wife:

> During the past year I have attempted to make love to you 365 times. I succeeded 36 times.

The rejection reasons listed are:

We'll wake the children. 7 times.
It's too hot. 15 times.
The windows are open and the neighbors will hear us.
   3 times.
You're too drunk. 9 times.
I'm not in the mood. 21 times.
Is that all you ever think about? 105 times.
      (Quoted in *Parade,* Nov. 15, 1970, p. 7.)

What the psychiatrist is revealing is the lack of a personal relationship even within marriage. But it is through such situations that the woman can become a prostitute and the man a John.

Marlene Nadle, in an article on the "Prostitute," quotes the description given by one prostitute of how she got into the "racket":

I started out working as a research assistant in a museum for seventy-seven fifty a week. I took home sixty-four dollars. I met a great many men on my job, so I got lots of date offers. I would take them as often as possible because any dinner I had out was one less dinner I had to pay for out of my salary.

And of course, most of them tried to sleep with me, and sometimes I did and sometimes I didn't, depending on how I felt about things. The ones I slept with acted as if they owned me, and the ones I didn't acted as though I was somehow cheating them.

Any way, my official change in status came one night when this guy took me to a very plush French restaurant. That must have cost him fifty dollars. Then he asked if I wanted to go on to a nite club. I was struck by the fact that this clod was spending more on the evening in the hopes of laying me than I earned all week.

At the time I was very broke, the rent was due, I hadn't bought anything new in god knows how long, and I was just drunk enough to say, "Look, what you really want is to go back to my place and screw me. What's the point of spending twenty or thirty dollars to watch a stupid floor show and all the time wonder whether or not I'll go to bed with you? Why not just give me the twenty dollars and we'll go straight back to my place?" Not too long after that I told the museum where to put their job and lawsamercy boss, things have never been the same since! . . .

They got their fun and I got dinner. Now I get paid and they get an act, a trick, an illusion. (*The Manhattan Tribune,* May 2, 1970, p. 13.)

The successful prostitute molds herself to fit the man's concept of her. She is an actress, and she acts the part that fits the audience.

Prostitution has always existed in the urban society, usually at several different levels. The rich can pay to keep one or more women free for their sexual use. Merchants, industrialists, and politicians are known to frequent the brothels of the "ports" they visit on business. Merchants also participate in the so-called white slave traffic. The poor worker or sailor uses his last pennies "for a night." Fathers take their sons to the prostitute in order to introduce them to sex.

The ideal Christian woman was to be like the Virgin Mary, to have her children without sex, to be the pure, sweet, bland mother, and to serve her husband as her Master and Provider. The young girl (and the young boy), according to this ideal, is told nothing about sex, and is warned about "those" girls, who are the ones the boys are interested in. The standard saying by the mother is that when it comes time to settle down, the boy-man will choose the "good" girl. The father tells the son to play around all he wants, but to choose a "good" woman for a wife. In fact, the father expects the "chip off the old block" to have sex with many different women. Otherwise he just isn't a man. The daughter, however, must remain a virgin.

Prostitution is much more the norm in Western society than

is admitted. The public today does not openly condone prostitution, but behind the scenes the prostitute is considered essential to the happy man.

Men learned early that prostitution could be a means for them to make a living. As mentioned before, merchants developed the white slave trade. They provided girls and women from all over the world to whoever would pay for them. Once established in a brothel or violated by a man by force, the woman would usually become a prostitute. This is partly a result of the degradation involved. But it also results from the owners of brothels holding the women forever in debt by making them dress well and by taking from the women at least 50 percent of the fee. Buying clothing, especially in the early years the woman is in the racket, appears to make the experience more bearable by keeping up an exterior appearance of well-being.

The slave traders have many different techniques for acquiring girls and women. Some go to the village or town and "rush" a girl. This rushing is explained to the girl as resulting from the pressure of time since the man must return to the city in a few days. Will she come with him? To every girl brought up to think a good marriage is her goal in life, being asked to come with the man to the city is guarantee of his sincerity, that this is not just a "summer romance." Once in the city, he takes her to her first client and tells her this is the only way they can get enough money to be married.

Another technique is to promise the woman a job. In such a situation frequently the parents give consent, for they cannot provide for the maturing girl or they feel she should have a job. Sometimes the women, even though married, will leave at the promise of a job that will pay enough to provide food and housing for their children. Even middle-class suburban housewives have become part-time prostitutes, perhaps out of boredom, out of a need to contribute to the household income, or out of an attempt to be independent persons.

Another means of the procurer is to promise girls an exciting life away from the drudgery of the factory or the home. He tells them outright that he will make them prostitutes, but that for a little work they can have much money, furs, and jewelry. The procurer may also promise women that they will have famous, prominent men as their clients.

The techniques can be innumerable, but the above illustrate the usual methods. The more ruthless of the procurers may use drugs and alcohol to force a girl or woman to give herself to prostitution.

Women as well as men work as procurers and brothel keepers. Sometimes the successful prostitutes move into the administration of the business. Their procurement techniques vary from those of the men mainly in that they emphasize persuasion with promises of money.

Another means to financial profit for a man in the prostitution business is to become a pimp. The relationship of pimp to prostitute is in many ways the complete reversal of the usual marital roles. The woman makes the money to keep her man, and he drives her on and on to make more money and to give it to him. She satisfies his every whim for material things, and bargains with him for his complete attention. He in turn visits her often, every night or every other night, depending on how many prostitutes he serves. He aims to make the prostitute psychologically dependent upon him. He knows the police and the underworld, and so claims to protect the prostitute from being taken advantage of, within the context of the profession. He is her only "reliable" contact. Otherwise she has no friends except other prostitutes, and no family. She has no enduring love relationship, only the mutual dependency with her pimp.

Men can gain indirect profits from prostitutes by holding

service jobs through which they learn of the women's professions. Where prostitution is illegal, service persons can charge higher prices, require bribes, or blackmail the "girls." As Polly Adler says in *A House Is Not a Home*:

> What it comes down to is this: the grocer, the butcher, the baker, the merchant, the landlord, the druggist, the liquor dealer, the policeman, the doctor, the city father and the politician—these are the people who make money out of prostitution, these are the real reapers of the wages of sin. (Adler, p. 309.)

These profits occur only where the threat of arrest and withdrawal of services can be held over the prostitute's or the madam's head. As a social outcast on the surface, yet an integral part of society in fact, the prostitute must pay for the illegality involved in the exterior. One cannot help wondering whether this front of opposition to "immorality" is for the sake of the conscience, or so that men can hide from their own problems.

The lowest grade of prostitution, according to those in the racket, or profession, is the streetwalker who depends upon drunken sailors and the derelicts of society as clients. She herself is a derelict in the sense that no one really wants her. She may have been a call girl at one time or a resident in a brothel. But then age, alcohol or drugs, and poverty overtook her. She could no longer retain the pretty mask. Her health has disintegrated and venereal disease has taken its ugly toll. Even societies in which a prostitute is highly respected and considered sacred hold the streetwalker in disrepute, and call her a "whore." Economic status seems to be the decisive factor in whether or not the prostitute is respected or is spat upon.

Whereas the streetwalker has to take what she can get for clients and for a fee, and because of this has to have scores of Johns a night in order to survive, though she is eventually killed by the process, the call girl has more security. She in essence has a business with lists of regular clients, knowledge of their likes and needs, and "respectable" references. The client of the call girl knows that she receives medical care and that she is selective in her customers. The upper-level call girl has taste and perhaps a well-developed intellect. She will go out on a date with her client, which allows him to pretend a personal relationship without the fear and strain of an actual relationship. He gets someone to show off who will in private serve his physical needs and make no demands on him except for his money. He does not have to feel guilty, since this was a business transaction and he paid the cost of the merchandise. (Men who take women on dates probably do not allow themselves to feel guilty, either, when they demand payment in the form of sexual relations.)

The madam of the call girl or of the brothel is even more the businesswoman, for she administers the successful sales transactions of her merchandise. She carefully selects the merchandise that she intends to sell, prices it as high as possible, giving it maximum value, guards it with concern, creates the atmosphere in which the buyer will feel relaxed and content, and then makes a successful sale. This is the higher-quality shop. And just as with stores, so there are a few houses of prostitution that are elegant and luxurious, the majority of houses are simply clean and have ordinary merchandise, and there are many that are literally ratholes.

At the pinnacle of prostitution is the courtesan, the geisha, the hetaerae. These women have become the heroines of their respective societies. They provide cultural and intellectual as well as physical intimacy. The hetaerae of ancient Greece knew well the philosophers, the statesmen, and the generals. Writers such as Diogenes, Pericles, Plato, and Praxiteles helped make them famous.

Courtesans of ancient Egypt are said to have built pyramids with the income they received from their clients. One legend, which we know through Herodotus, claims that Cheops' daughter became a courtesan and demanded from each client one stone, and out of these stones she built two pyramids.

Women slaves in the ancient world could best gain freedom and status by becoming courtesans. Frequently women who were slaves had become so only through war and so might have received a good education. The woman in a strange land could achieve nothing with an education, but education allied with sex could be the way to success, wealth, and influence.

Apparently ancient rulers as well as recent rulers spent more time with their courtesans than with their wives. But the transactions during these meetings generally have not been considered important by historians, and we are left with no sense of how much influence individual women may have had upon the early rulers. The records for specific later rulers are somewhat better, but until historians actually recognize the abilities of women and the power that women attained through sexual bargaining, we shall have no idea of the full extent of the influence of women upon history.

The French courtesans, especially those who gained renown in the eighteenth century, tended to come from the lower nobility or from the educated, but not the wealthy middle class. These women generally had gained proficiency in the classics, in philosophy, and in theology, but they had nowhere to go but to tutor the children of the rich, a not particularly satisfying task. And in such a position, the woman would be at the mercy of the master of the house and his friends and might well have to prostitute herself. The role of courtesan, or of head of a *salon*, could not fail to attract the young, intelligent, aspiring woman. The two positions—courtesan and head of a *salon*— did not necessarily overlap, though frequently the woman in

demand was in demand both intellectually and sexually. And
if she herself did not fill the sexual role, other women in her
salon did.

The difficulties for an intellectual woman are illustrated in
Marie Meurdrac's Foreword to her treatise on chemistry:

> I objected to myself that it was not the profession of a
> lady to teach; that she should remain silent, listen and
> learn, without displaying her own knowledge; that it is
> above her station to offer a work to the public and that a
> reputation gained thereby is not ordinarily to her advan-
> tage since men always scorn and blame the products of a
> woman's wit. And furthermore, such secrets perhaps
> should not be divulged; that because of the inadequacy of
> my description, many things may have to be revised.
> (Bishop and DeLoach, quoted from Marie Meurdrac, "La
> Chymie charitable et facile, en faveur des dames," 1680.)

She goes on to explain why women should publish their work,
while stating that she realizes what little chance she has to
succeed with her own work. (It was only in 1969 that this essay
was "discovered" and brought to the attention of chemists.)

The women who have made some impact on historians are
the courtesans and mistresses to government leaders. Perhaps
best known among these are Mlle. d'Entragues (whose family
received 100,000 crowns from Henry IV, then married to Mar-
garet of Navarre), Mme. de Montespan (who bore Louis XIV
seven children), Mme. de Maintenon, Mme. de Tencin
(mother of d'Alembert, the French mathematician and philoso-
pher), Mme. Pompadour, and Mme. du Barry. As noted in
Section II, some of these women used magic, mainly in the
form of love potions, to maintain their positions, for they could
not depend upon intellect and sex alone.

More recently the Profumo affair in England brought to the
attention of the public the involvement of government officials

with today's equivalent of the eighteenth-century courtesan.

In September, 1970, the press carried the story of Marie Veraeke, who at age seventeen was in a Belgian convent training to become a nurse. Eugenio Messina courted her at the convent for five years, and then by offering to marry her, took her to London. There she was forced, at gun point, to marry an Englishman, through which process she gained English citizenship. From 1954 to 1960 the Messinas forced her to work as a prostitute. When exiled in 1960, Eugenio took Marie to Italy. They lived together for ten years and then married on March 12, 1970, the day Eugenio died. Over this period the five Messina brothers amassed about fifty million dollars' profit from prostitution.

In some countries it is estimated that as many as one in ten women are prostitutes. Government leaders, industrialists, and bankers, as well as salesmen, soldiers, and sailors visit the local prostitutes while on "business," and the former discount the cost on their expense accounts. For centuries, governments have kept prostitutes, both directly and indirectly. Just as the sheik would share his harem with a guest, so a government official or businessman in entertaining a colleague will take him to a prostitute or a brothel, the purpose being "good business relationships."

Governments learned long ago to employ prostitutes as spies or to have their spies be prostitutes. Again the role of the woman is to seduce the man and gain power over him through sex. In some countries this is the only opening in government service for women, since men are used as clerks and secretaries as well as leaders. Such is the kind of security and power allowed women by male governments. For a woman to play such a game is to walk a tightrope, and the penalty for failure must be the same as for all spies: death. Just as the Crusades and the church councils had their prostitute traveling companions, so do government officials and businessmen today. And if the man is not particularly well off, the secretary who goes along for business must double as sexual partner.

Governments indirectly encourage prostitution by not providing equal employment opportunity for women and by allowing tax monies to be used to continue sexism in the public schools. (Cf. Pennsylvania Department of Education *Report of the Joint Task Force on Sexism in Education,* 1972.) Women do not receive any special tax rate, and under the U.S. tax system, the people at the bottom of the ladder pay a much higher portion of their income to the state than do the persons at the top. Since women are at the very bottom of the income ladder, they bear the heaviest brunt of taxation, while the Johns deduct their expenses from their taxable income.

Prostitutes clearly bear the traits of the oppressed. They live the misogynists' descriptions of women, the characteristics ascribed to women by the churches. Prostitutes seek out men for sexual intercourse. They ply their trade at theaters, in lobbies, in restaurants, on the street.

In prostitution the extropunitive Traits Due to Victimization appear most readily to the observer. But in fact the intropunitive traits are found more frequently. A prostitute, especially one below the call-girl level, has to have clients and so seeks her Johns. All prostitutes have to manipulate the men, for that is what is expected. In the past year a few incidents of role reversal have occurred: rather than the prostitute being robbed by the John, the John has been robbed or beaten up by one or more prostitutes. This is sly, cunning, aggressive, in-group behavior.

The most overwhelming characteristic of the prostitute, though, is her self-hate. She becomes what she "looks," and she can always cover up or hide who she is. In the most intimate of interpersonal acts, she must feel nothing. She molds herself to the likes and dislikes of the individual John. She becomes an outcast, cut off by family, harassed by the police, the victim of every blackmailer.

The sex role as prostitute is inevitable in a society that has the attitudes toward women described throughout this book. Women become prostitutes for many reasons, some of which come from women's desires to be accepted, and many of which are the result of the attitudes toward women and the self-perceptions of women, which in turn are institutionalized in the sexism in education and employment practices.

3. Marriage, Mistresses, and Intrigue

Some prostitutes serve as mistresses from time to time. Some mistresses formally marry. Some wives act as mistresses. Some mistresses make polygamy possible without the legal entanglements. And according to the interpretations of some persons, all marriage is prostitution. Because of the oppression of women, most of them partake of various kinds of intrigue, especially when they are seeking the security of a marriage. In many arrangements between a woman and a man, the woman withholds or grants sexual intercourse according to what she is trying to obtain. Because of the attitudes toward and the position of women in all male-dominated countries, this is her greatest power.

Prostitution is considered better than a permanent sexual arrangement by many women. For a prostitute to settle down with a John is unusual, though it does happen. But in such cases the assistance of a psychiatrist is crucial, and extreme patience by the man involved is necessary. The prostitute has to learn that the man cares about her as a person. She cannot marry without this, and often her marriage will be more enduring than the usual marriage which is based on the convenience of sex.

Marriage is basically a legal arrangement, and it may or may not include a real involvement of two people in each other's lives. Many marriages simply legalize the mistress relationship or the ancient slave relationship, or they provide for prostitution with one man. So long as the marriage consists of the woman's being kept for the man's pleasure, this is true. And considering the British psychiatrist's findings that marriages collapse mainly because of the woman withdrawing from sexual intimacies, it would appear that sex does play the major role in marital relationships. The psychiatrist neglects the underlying reasons for the woman's withdrawal. But I suspect that the distinction between marriage and prostitution is not in the quantity of sex, but in the way sex is used between two persons—to gratify sexual desires, to have power over someone, or to communicate the depth of feeling the woman and the man have for each other. Prostitution must be without feeling. (The prostitute who feels becomes terrified and has to leave the profession.) It is a job for which the woman receives her income. Marriage, on the other hand, ideally is a bond between two people who are equal. Marriage and prostitution, by these definitions, undoubtedly overlap in practice, for the kept married woman is more the norm than the exception.

When women try to gain wealth, security, influence, and even power by making sexual arrangements, their action is tantamount to prostitution, at least at first, but the action is also an expression of the training the woman has received in her social upbringing. The woman must make a good marriage. With women's liberation is coming a change in the socializing of both women and men. Attempts to enforce laws that prohibit sex discrimination in employment also assist the freeing of women from purely sex roles. Now it is becoming acceptable in most Western countries for a woman to develop her intellectual and leadership potentials in order to participate fully in the society. In societies that do not allow such participation, the marriage of a woman is crucial to her success and to her survival, unless she is heir to an estate or to a throne.

To arrange a successful marriage is impossible for most women. Their families or protectors must accomplish this. When the family is wealthy and powerful, it will negotiate well for power and status but not for the happiness of the daughter.

Catherine of Aragon, wife of Arthur, Prince of Wales, and then of Henry VIII of England, exemplifies this well. Catherine was the daughter of Ferdinand and Isabella of Spain, and so the marriage to the heir to the throne of England produced a diplomatic bond between Spain and England. Catherine was expected to be the link between Spain and England, and the bond between her father and mother and her husband. The marriage itself was secondary. But as the wife of the king, Catherine had to produce male heirs. Much as she had been trained to administer a kingdom and to run a household, she had not learned how to produce male heirs. Only one of her six children survived infancy, and this one was female. Meanwhile Luther had posted his Ninety-five Theses on the church door in Wittenberg, and the alliance between Henry and Charles V, Catherine's nephew, collapsed. Henry began moving in new directions away from the old diplomatic alliances to gain his strength and independence, and Catherine was no part of the new direction. But Henry could not get rid of her by her own consent. She held firm her convictions without the support of any of the persons who had put her into the situation in the first place—her father, her mother, and her husband and his advisers. Catherine had been a pawn in the men's world of politics, and she had been unable to use her sex to manipulate herself into a position of power. Her failure in motherhood meant political failure. She died, ill, sorrowful, and alone.

Prior to the twentieth century, to have a daughter was to be overly burdened, even to be cursed. The daughter could not carry on the family name. She could not rise to power. Sacred and secular prostitution provided one solution to the problem, for in this way the daughter could be used to make men happy and could be kept out of trouble; the convent provided another; marriage, a third. All three "solutions" could produce death within ten years: by physical decay, by vegetating in boredom, and by childbirth.

But some women were tough and made the best of the situation for their own power and satisfaction. One such woman was Catherine de Medici, who outlived her husband and her children, and gained the pinnacle of power in sixteenth-century France. Catherine, daughter of Lorenzo de Medici, Duke of Urbino, married the Duke of Orleans (later Henry II) in 1533. During her husband's reign she did not publicly exercise power, but by the time her second son, Charles IX, became king in 1560, she was powerful enough to have herself named regent. Though balancing off the various religious factions during the first two years of her regency, in 1562 Catherine identified with the Catholics, the family of Guise. Then when her influence over her son was threatened, she attempted to have the culprit, Coligny, assassinated. With the Guise faction she planned the massacre of the Huguenots on St. Bartholomew's Day in 1572. She continued to devote her political talents to power plays until her death in 1589.

Marriage provided an in for Catherine de Medici which otherwise would have been available to her only through the less legal means of prostitution. And through marriage she was able to come closer to the throne than could a man not of the royal family. Catherine's own family experiences certainly gave her some status and bargaining power, but as a female member of the Medici family she could never have achieved the plateau she maintained during the last part of her life as widow and mother of kings.

Lucretia Borgia had experiences during her childhood similar to those of Catherine de Medici. Her family controlled popes and monarchs and played politics all over Europe. Lucretia did not marry into power, however. But her name did become synonymous with treachery and manipulation. Even then aspiring rulers could not deny their fascination with her as through her sex and her intellect she controlled them. The more that men who thought they could gain the Borgia power through her sought after her, the more powerful she became. Through her sex role, she managed to gain extensive political leverage.

Lady Bird Johnson had money and status in her own right, through her family, much as did Lucretia Borgia. She married a man without wealth and power, Lyndon Baines Johnson, and the two together amassed considerable money and influence. Lyndon Baines Johnson became President of the United States, and, according to all accounts, depended heavily on Ms. Johnson's intellect and psychological strength. They apparently had worked out a relationship which made it possible for her to advise him and even to oppose his positions, though she never publicly spoke any criticism of him, and she developed the characteristics of the proper middle-class American woman concerned with her dress and her role as hostess. Ms. Johnson never set herself up as a political power which had to be contended with, which was quite the opposite of the patterns established by Catherine and Lucretia.

The wife of Richard M. Nixon, on the other hand, sometimes has appeared either to have been cast aside by her husband or to have withdrawn completely into her concept of the middle-class American woman as servant, hostess, and mother. The Pat Nixon who by the second year of her husband's presidency was holding sewing circles for the wives of cabinet members appeared to have lost her personhood. Her trips to the U.S.S.R. and the Republic of China, however, revealed a capable, intelligent, independent woman.

Other women, especially those who had no family to arrange a marriage, sought their ends through sexually attracting powerful men. These women led the shaky life of "mistress." If the man were very old, little in the way of actual sexual relations was involved. Just the presence of a pretty young body for seeing and touching might be enough. In other cases a husband might arrange for his wife to become someone's mistress as a means of gaining favor. Or, the king himself might make and break marriages in order to gain control of a woman, most probably actions encouraged by the women involved.

Most rulers and wealthy men have several women at their beck and call. For the women, this is always their chance and it is their only hope for success. For the man, having such apparent power over women gives him a sense of well-being.

King Louis XIV is especially well known for his mistresses, including Mlle. de La Vallière and Mme. de Montespan. He might desire any woman around, and if he did not obtain her immediately, she or her husband or family would be banned and their livelihood destroyed. The man at court, too, found wife-swapping and having mistresses a major pastime. Petty intrigues were encouraged by Louis, for it left him with the real power. It is in a situation such as this, with such complete intrigue and manipulation, that clever women have their best opportunities for power.

Louis XV followed in Louis XIV's tracks with mistresses who have become even more famous, Mmes. Pompadour and du Barry. Mme. Pompadour first served Louis XV as his mistress

for about five years and during that time gained his confidence,
so that when she fell from sexual favor, she continued to be
his confidante. Since she was of middle-class origin, the path of
the *salons* was a normal direction for her to move in. She
knew the intellectuals of the time and she patronized the arts,
especially as she could use artists to decorate her many resi-
dences.

Marie Jeanne Bécu du Barry did not have the experience of
the *salons*. She moved more directly from courtesan, which
status she had reached through her patron Jean du Barry, to
becoming mistress to the king. Whereas Mme. Pompadour had
served Louis from 1745 to 1750, Mme. du Barry became his
mistress for the last six years of his life, 1768–1774. Upon Louis'
death, she retired from court, but so much did the Revolutionaries fear her intrigues that they had her guillotined in
1793. How else than through sexual means could a nameless
woman of illegitimate birth have become such a threat?

Napoleon Bonaparte, intending to end court intrigues, had
also to prevent women from gaining the stature of the mistresses and courtesans of the kings. So he married Josephine,
whose actions and appearance typify the dumb-blond sexpot
of more recent times. She kept out of the affairs of state and
concentrated on social affairs. Napoleon had the marriage annulled because of Josephine's apparent sterility, only to marry
another woman immediately—reminiscences of Henry VIII.

As throughout Europe the royal family was moved out of
power, government decisions became even more completely
the prerogative of men who left their wives and mistresses to
act only in the role of hostess and in bed. Court intrigue had
been severely curtailed and women's roles became even more
restricted to those of mother and sex object.

Today the role of the court mistress (not necessarily sexual)
has reappeared, though more subtly than it existed in the eight-

eenth century. Anna Chennault, for example, lives in the un-official Nixon government's residence, the Watergate Apartments, where she occupies a luxurious penthouse. She has free access to U.S. government officials, to President Thieu, to President Marcos, and to President Chiang Kai-shek, and knows all the right people, especially in the military. She is not on the official payroll of any government. In 1968 she even campaigned for Nixon-Agnew—as a celebrity. In 1972 she was vice-chair*man* of the Platform Committee for the Republican Party. She has been one of the few women in political campaigns who are considered worth more than the volunteer labor for canvassing and stuffing envelopes.

The sexual role as wife or mistress reveals patterns similar to those of the prostitute. Overall the pace is easier, so the woman is not destroyed as quickly. The wife and the mistress usually make some demands on the man and can use withholding of sex as a means to obtain these demands. The prostitute cannot do this because sex is her income. Many wives and mistresses are at the mercy of their husbands or lovers, for they are terrified of being left, of having to make it on their own.

The manipulative power- or money-seeking wives and mistresses carry the extropunitive Traits Due to Victimization. Those who submit to all the wishes and demands of their husbands and children, denying their own existence as persons, show mainly the intropunitive traits.

The relationship that allows the two persons to be equal, to respect each other, to share and to cooperate, is unique. In such a relationship women are not subverted, and as a result they do not need to manipulate their husbands or lovers or to deny themselves full personhood.

4. The Working Woman and Sex

Polly Adler, the famous New York City madam of the 1930's, did not find her way into prostitution via marriage or a successful venture at being a mistress. Her skill was not in devious intrigue and the gaining of power through manipulating a male figurehead. She found her way into prostitution through her experiences in a factory where she had to sleep with the foreman in order to retain her job. As noted in the section on prostitution, several call girls who allowed themselves to be interviewed by various authors stated that they had seen no point in working a forty-hour week as a secretary and having to give after-hour sexual performances, all for a minimal salary, when for fewer working hours they could live more comfortably. To them both situations were degrading, and the lesser of the two evils appeared to be prostitution, for at least the hypocrisy (of one kind) would be gone and the income would provide a living wage. Why pretend? You may as well get paid for what you have to do anyway in order to keep a job.

The process of industrialization kept men in all the positions of authority. It left women in the positions of lowest status and pay, and even when men did hold the same low positions, they received more pay. So women worked in mines, in factories, and in sweat shops. And the greatest threat the male boss had over them was to take away the small pittance they received.

As the early trade union histories reveal, the men in authority had numerous means to cut off workers. Generally unemployment was always high, so no worker, especially not an unskilled woman worker, had any bargaining power. No matter where a woman went, if she were under the authority of a man, she ran the risk of having to pay sexually for whatever she wanted, be it a job, a chance for an education, a husband, or food for her children.

Because women could be hired as cheap labor and because men thought that men ought to have first choice of jobs, union organizers did not invite women to join. In this way even the male workers set themselves up in competition with women for positions, and looked down on women as a sort of scab labor. Very few countries witnessed any large-scale trade union organizing of women workers. The men organized and struck and eventually signed agreements with the bosses to obtain promotions, salary increases, and better working conditions. Through this process women became more firmly entrenched in the lower echelons of the labor force. Today the largest body of workers who still are not organized are the women secretaries. The male image of woman does not allow for outward militancy or toughness. The toughness that women have has come more subtly with the acceptance of oppression and endurance of all that the boss hands out.

One of the few channels open to the educated woman, as noted before—that of tutoring the children of the well-to-do— also frequently included sexual payment to the father. Teaching has now become an acceptable profession for women, but even here the men serve as the top administrators and as the majority of principals. Wages in the teaching profession have been raised only since the community decided it was bad for the children to have just women teachers, especially in high school: if students are to be prepared for successful careers, they must have male teachers, and male teachers must receive a living wage. Otherwise no incentive exists for the man to enter the teaching profession. Women did not organize teacher unions when the members of the profession on the precollege level were predominantly women. Again, they accepted the male image that they should be passive and should serve people.

Much as the majority of women accepted and lived out their

oppression, the clever woman would work out means to take advantage of any intimate opportunities with the male boss. She would bargain with him and eventually gain influence, if only in familiarity. Such a woman would occur a maximum of one in one hundred women workers. And she would soon fall from power, detested by her fellow workers, for there is no room for a woman in the upper levels of the industrial hierarchy.

The career woman today learns that she must play the game by male rules, and must be far better than any man around in order to succeed. But she must also appear to be filling the role of the submissive woman, for if she treats men as equals, they will be threatened by her abilities which most probably are superior. Part of the male rules referred to here are the sexist comments about women and the telling of sexual jokes. Women must not tell the jokes, but they must laugh at their own expense. They must also take in their stride the sexual oppression of other women used and bragged about by their male colleagues. As a result, many career women begin to dress in a masculine manner and to drop the female image, for their male counterparts can so thoroughly isolate them that the only way they have any companionship is to "become a man," be "one of the guys."

One woman in a large urban university who is known to this author completely conforms outwardly to the image the men have of women. She is the top woman administrator at the university and the only woman member of the executive decision-making body. She acts very sweet and demure around the men. She never says anything without looking at the men for permission. She waits for a man to light her cigarette. She does nothing that is not in complete coherence with the expressed and insinuated attitudes and policies of the men. She openly claims she "knows the male mind," so other women should leave everything up to her: "Women only hurt their own cause by making demands and openly seeking equality."

5. The Sex Role of Women in Education

For centuries only men received formal education. The Greek and the Roman schools and academies consisted mainly of male faculty and students. When the church took over education, it left women even more bereft of the possibilities of education since women simply were not allowed in the church hierarchy except as nuns and virgins. With the development of royal families and middle-class families, parents did frequently engage tutors for their daughters as well as for their sons. But the newly developing universities had little room for women, though the students were expected to frequent the local prostitutes and to install women in their rooms for their sexual pleasure. In this the university completely exemplified the attitudes of the church toward women. Oxford and Cambridge have allowed women students only in the last decade. Yet even in the fifteenth century, they were granting scholarships to poor men in order to allow them the opportunity for advancement.

Today when riots occur on campuses, so long as they are panty raids and invasions of the girls' living quarters the community considers it a joke. But when the riots involve persons protesting political and social acts and policies, the public is ready to close down the campuses.

The universities reflect this attitude of acceptance of the use of women as pawns in their policies and their treatment of women students, faculty, and staff. Women students have to have higher qualifications than men students to enter graduate schools. Fewer women than men obtain scholarships. Married women have difficulty gaining fellowships. Few child care and development facilities exist. Many women are refused faculty positions because their husbands teach, or are refused with no reason given. Some women are told they belong at home with their children or that they should get married—stick to their sex roles. In interviews women are asked, if they are not married, when they are getting married; if they are married, when they will have children; if they have children, when they will go through menopause. No matter where a woman is in terms of her life-span, she is verbally sexually assaulted in 99 percent of the interviews conducted by academic men.

Then there is the more direct sexual assault made by academic men on women under the threat of loss of job or failure in a course. I have known several women who have submitted sexually to professors because they believed there was nowhere they could go to prevent the professor from destroying them academically. One woman, propositioned in front of other students, refused and then was forced out of the department in which she was enrolled in a Ph.D. program. Other women live in constant fear of being drawn into a trap by a professor. A psychology professor, a former colleague of mine, made a practice of keeping pillows and blankets in his office and spending weekends there with women students.

For the women this is their one chance to be noticed, to be "valued," to be accepted. Recognition for their academic work is lacking. Being chosen by the professor sexually can be viewed as success.

The educational "subversion of women" begins for the female child when she learns that her mother is responsible for the satisfaction of her needs. Even if the mother works, she makes the arrangements and does whatever is necessary for the satisfaction of needs at home. Child care and development facilities do not exist except on an exceedingly minimal level, and then usually not for children under the age of three. If the mother is working, the child frequently is made to feel that something is wrong with the family and so the child needs special sympathy.

Then the child begins to look at books. Recently a major publisher released a book for small children describing what a girl does and what a boy does. The girl cooks; the boy eats. The girl is a nurse; the boy, a doctor. And so forth. The mother in children's stories usually cooks the meals, does the housework, the washing, and the ironing. She may also work, but if she does, she is seen prettily sitting at a typewriter or standing at a filing cabinet. But the father goes off to work, to his business where he is an important executive with the weight of major decisions. Men are also shown doing interesting jobs working with machines and laboratory equipment. The woman may be shown as a teacher, a librarian, or a nurse, but certainly not as a pilot, an astronaut, a government official, or a member of the board.

The children reveal through their ditties and jokes their concepts of each other. The sayings of young children, which are sexually oriented, make fun of female organic functions, especially of the breasts. At costume parties in schools, boys will frequently dress up with pillows as bosoms. I have never yet heard of a girl dressed up with a penis. She would be told she had penis envy and her parents would be told the child was seriously ill mentally and should be taken to a psychiatrist, if not to a mental institution. When the girl reaches high school, she becomes a cheerleader or majorette and wears short skirts so the men will watch her. She is there to gain support for the male players.

The schools in the United States have very limited education in human sexuality, when there is any at all. As a result, if a picture of a pregnant woman or animal, or a picture of a baby animal or child suckling the mother is shown, snickers spread through the classroom.

These examples simply point out the attitudes toward women and toward sex in our society which are inculcated in young children. The woman is servant, mother, and sex object. The man has important functions and can use the woman sexually whenever he wants, with no concern for her as a person or for her feelings. Women are not supposed to have feelings. This attitude becomes reality in the relationship of the John to the prostitute.

6. Women and War

Women have served as the spoils of war and the declared reasons for war throughout history.

In the wars of the Greeks and the Romans, the civilians of the losing side became slaves to the victors. They were claimed by the soldiers themselves as their due or were sold in the marketplace. Today the victors do not take slaves, but they rape whatever women are around. To the male victor, this is the ultimate degradation of the male loser—to take his wife or mother or daughter sexually. Soldiers have always done this, and the situation in Vietnam has been no different. It was only more complex because of the length of the war, the quantity of soldiers and fighting personnel, and the intensity and strength of the weapons.

As Americans, for example, moved as a military power into a strange land and culture in Vietnam, they totally disrupted the economy of the country and the life of the people. The Americans became the occupation forces who lived off the land, which included the women who live on that land. The Americans accomplished total disruption not only by the bombing and military devastation but also by the new consumers market and the new money which they brought with them. As people lost their homes and their means of livelihood, they drifted toward the cities and the army camps. The Americans, isolated from the Vietnamese people by language barriers, propaganda, and barbed wire, sought to escape their homesickness and their fear. Women began to fill places where liquor was sold. The managers of such places didn't take long to recognize the financial gain in serving women and sex with drinks. And so the thriving business in prostitution and mistresses developed. The women would do anything for an American dollar. This could buy food for a child.

Those women who became mistresses had relatively more security than the regular prostitute, but they also usually ended up having a child. Still the soldier would "keep" her and that was better than starving. The crucial decision time came, though, when the soldier was recalled. What about the woman, and perhaps the child? The U.S. Government made the marriage of a GI with a Vietnamese woman very difficult, even when members of the Government themselves made prostitutes out of Vietnamese women. So even if the GI did want to marry the woman, the Government did not want her or their child as immigrants to the United States. Yet because these Vietnamese women were degraded by becoming prostitutes or mistresses to Americans, they received no respect in Vietnam and so they became desperate with fear and would do anything in order to marry the GI.

The Vietnamese man shuns the woman who has prostituted herself to the American and shuns the child of such a union. The women are left with no livelihood, for only the Americans had money. There are few jobs for the prostitute or the ex-prostitute, and no child care and development centers for the working woman should she be able to find a job. Even the older women who have served the GI's nonsexually lose their jobs. The stores must close. Poverty and unemployment increase.

Nguyen Thi Khao, a forty-one-year-old woman who worked for American GI's, was interviewed by *The New York Times*.

She lives with her husband, a disabled veteran, and six children (the oldest of whom are the same age as the GIs) about half a mile from the base camp, where she has worked for four years.

"It's a shame to talk about my salary," she said in Vietnamese. "It is only 4,000 piasters a month and there has been no raise in pay since I have been here." At the legal rate of exchange, her monthly salary is about $33.

"Every day I make up the beds in the rooms of seven soldiers, wash their clothes—combat fatigues, underwear, socks, handkerchiefs—iron the uniforms, sweep the floors and keep everything in their rooms clean." . . .

Her husband, who was a corporal, receives a pension of about $8 per month. . . .

"My husband stays home to look after the younger children—there is a one-year-old baby—and raise pigs, five pigs," she continued, "but food for pigs is very expensive now. Of course there are mountains of thrown-out food but I may not take it because there is a contractor who is the only one allowed to collect the garbage."

Her salary is enough to buy the rice her family needs every month.

The article continues:

Vietnamese women are also hired to clean the kitchens and wash the pots and pans in the mess halls, to wait on tables where officers sit and to serve as bar girls in the clubs on the base and as manual laborers who are paid by the day to fill sandbags, pick up litter and dig ditches. Except for the laborers, most of the women are young, prone to primping and quick to giggle.

Ms. Khao noted:

"You know, . . . American soldiers have much money and it seems that they are all sexually hungry all the time.

Our poor girls. With money and a little patience, the Americans can get them very easily. There is violent resistance at first, but then, well, you know." (*The New York Times*, June 5, 1970, p. 4.)

So for a short time the women in a war-torn area could survive, some even becoming relatively well off economically by serving sexually the foreign and domestic soldiers. But this well-being was short-lived, either by the ending of the war, which the women lose no matter what the military outcome, or by their own self-destruction. Medical facilities in war areas can hardly be used to treat the women who serve as the sexual objects of the occupying soldiers, especially not when people are having their insides blown out and their skin burned by napalm, and children are being deformed by the various antipersonnel weapons. Today only four hundred doctors serve South Vietnam's seventeen million civilians. (*The New York Times*, Sept. 14, 1972.)

What about the wives left in the United States? Were they supposed to sit around at home almost starving on the income provided by their soldier-husbands who were in Vietnam presumably to "protect" them? Many women did sit at home, lonely and miserable. Others could not, for their personalities and their mental health motivated them to participate actively in the world around them. The loneliness, the need to belong, and sexual needs tended to drive them into another relationship, or even into prostitution.

One wonders what is the cause of all the destruction and suffering that is brought on so many people. In her column, Flora Lewis suggested that government officials' concern for their "manhood" and insecurity might be the real cause of the continuation of the Vietnam war.

The day before President Nixon sent U.S. troops into Cambodia, which was a day after he had made that decision, a high-level White House adviser was discussing the President's problems with a visitor.

"He's got to show America hasn't lost its manhood," the aide said. "Our manhood can't be left in question."

And indeed, the President did refer to that theme in his speech, though he used other words. He warned against the U.S. acting "like a pitiful helpless giant." (*Pittsburgh Post-Gazette,* May 13, 1970, p. 8.)

Everyone has heard fathers telling their sons that the Army "will make a man out of you." The insinuation seems to be dual: sexual in terms of learning to use women more freely and sexual in terms of learning to fire a gun. The assumption is that it takes more guts to kill than not to kill. Dropping bombs on civilians, massacring women and children, maiming thousands of people, takes courage. Flora Lewis suggests that this "is the opposite of noble strength."

The above description of the war in Vietnam applies basically to every war. The government officials continue to proclaim the necessity of the war to "protect our women and children." They are horrified at the thought of women in the army, though the underground and the U.S.S.R. used women extensively in World War II, and the Vietnamese National Liberation Front, North Vietnam, Israel, and China all have women soldiers today. Yet, in reality, how could having the ability to defend oneself, to shoot back, make the situation worse for the women than is the situation described above which exists in every occupied territory? Masculinity has become synonymous with the gun and the penis. And both are to be used to destroy.

Hitler's use of women in World War II is a more blatant use of sex as a means to control people than is seen under most war conditions. Hitler and the SS troops took Jewish women and set them up in brothels for the German soldiers' use, and made the women work until they died, which was usually in a few days. Non-Jewish German women also had to provide for the

German soldiers. Any sign of refusal meant that the woman was a traitor, for Hitler had called upon all women to serve their country through motherhood. Some individual women, such as Hitler's mistress, Eva Braun, did rise to prominence through their services to the officers, but the majority just had to become patriots by their ability to have intercourse.

7. Sex and Race

Besides being able to survive in a war situation by means of sexual relations (when not allowed to fight), women have also maintained themselves by having sexual intercourse with persons of another race. Just as in war when the woman at the mercy of the soldier will offer sex for survival, so the woman of the oppressed race will offer sex to the master. This obviously is not a one-way transaction: the man involved has usually expressed his desire, or even demand, for the offer.

Both types of transactions are highly dangerous for the woman, since the man has superior power and could destroy her. To be successful, she must outsmart and manipulate him. There is also in this, for the man especially, something of the unreality involved in going to the professional prostitute. He can lose his inhibition and really "enjoy" sex, so he thinks, for it does not entail any personal involvement. It is exciting because it is different, and it is a marvelous sense of power.

Whereas the wife is worried about bills, housing, children, schools, the job, the neighbors, the woman having only sexual contact will not voice any such concerns. (This is not to say there cannot be forthright interracial marriages. The level of oppression of the woman is a determining factor and most marriages, interracial or not, are based on oppression.)

The man of the oppressed race who has an affair with the

woman of the master race is in a particularly dangerous position. The woman is also oppressed and so may be seeking a way to retaliate against the man or men of her race. The woman is also considered the master's property in a way the master is never the property of the woman. Thus the oppressed man is stealing the master's property. (The woman of the master race never views the woman of the oppressed race as stealing her property.) He is also turning against the women of his race. And he does not hesitate to send "his woman" to the master if it will help him, just as families and husbands have sold their daughters and wives for centuries.

As victims of oppression, it is possible that the women of the master race receive pleasure in having sexual relations with oppressed men, since it gives them a sense of revenge against their owners, the men of the master race. Also, through the intropunitive traits of the oppressed, they may identify with oppressed people. Yet the identity is allowable usually only with the men, not the women, for social training has bred into both men and women the attitude that all women are inferior, not even people with whom one can identify. Punishment of the "master," however, does appear to be a main motivation, as one call girl told a psychiatrist: "I paid a black man fifty dollars to have intercourse with me just to get back at my pimp."

The court history of the South in the United States is filled with trials and lynchings of black men accused of raping white women. There is no equivalent court history of trials of black women, of white men, or of white women. Clearly, what white men do is considered legitimate and black and white women are simply the pawns of the men involved.

In the '50s in Hawaii, the wife of a U.S. naval officer claimed she had been raped by four to six Hawaiians. Four young men were arrested as a result, and one was allegedly killed by the husband of the woman. A trial was held. The white naval officer was found guilty of murder but received no punishment. The charges against the three remaining Hawaiians were dropped for lack of evidence. And nobody dared charge the white woman with lying. The entire story has never been revealed, but whatever happened, the white man and woman escaped by means of placing accusations of rape against persons of another race. (Doctors did not find any signs of rape.) (Theon Wright, *Rape in Paradise*; Hawthorn Books, 1966.)

A few years ago during New Left meetings militant blacks were beating up and having intercourse with willing white women. Today black men are heard to say they like white women because they make a man feel good. The black separatists decry this attitude. Black women are angry with white women for allowing black men to desert black women. The black men apparently are motivated to take white women in order to revenge the acts of white men in the past, just as white women have taken revenge on white men by using black men. And the white women may now be trying to gain influence and control over both black and white men in power in the traditional way of becoming the woman behind the man.

In the past, black women have had on the average an education equivalent to that of black men. In difficult times black women could get a job, menial as it might have been, when the black man could find nothing. But in the last few years, with the progress of the civil rights movement, black men have gained top-level positions, but black women have risen to equality with white women only as secretaries. The income scales for the United States reveal the white man on top, then the black man; third, the white woman; and on the bottom, the black woman.

And as the black men oppress black women, they also accuse the women of not liking black men. "Liking" here appears to mean willingness to adopt the intropunitive traits, imitating the pattern of the white middle-class woman. Such an accusation shatters the self-identity of the woman as black. Men, black and white, are in the power structure. Women are not. White women use sex. At present black women cannot, except as prostitutes, since they were never made into unattainable "Virgin Marys" on pedestals. And the American society is pushing black women to emulate white women in becoming submissive, yet manipulative, and calculating in their use of sex. After all, manhood must be defined by sex and the black man has been deprived of his "manhood" by the white man.

8. Sexual Relations and Law Enforcement

Recently a major network television news broadcaster reported the situation of a town in Nebraska that had been receiving a $1,000-per-month payoff from a brothel owner. The town officials had decided to license the brothel at the cost of $1,000 per month. The mayor reported this action as bringing great relief to his conscience.

Germany and several other European countries have legalized prostitution and require all prostitutes to have regular medical checkups. But the majority of countries in the world, though they have a thriving prostitution trade, refuse to legalize it.

In past centuries the English government tried to keep lists of women prostitutes, but they had no means of proving prostitution and granted an accused woman no trial or appeal. By the end of the nineteenth century, whoever made out the lists included whomever *he* wanted. The lists provided men in the community with access to prostitutes and publicly ostracized the accused women, so that to survive at all they had to become prostitutes. The lists took from the prostitute any chance she might have had to screen her customers. And the threat of being put on the list made women in general subject to much abuse. This aspect runs parallel to the threat of witchcraft accusations in earlier centuries.

Many doctors who examined prostitutes were not careful and sometimes damaged the patient. Not knowing or caring about germs, they did not clean the speculum but used the same one for one examination after another, in this manner transferring venereal disease. A woman found with venereal disease was immediately put in a hospital, sometimes several miles away, without being allowed to try to arrange for her home or her children. Again she had no recourse and no appeal. And she could not leave the hospital until the authorities gave their permission.

The officials also set up a particular time and place for the examination of the women on the list. If a woman did not show up, she was brought by force. The administrators of these laws seem to have had great drives to have women publicly exhibited, examined internally, and incarcerated.

No attempt was made in England or in any other country that I know of, except the U.S.S.R., to end prostitution by opening up employment, equal opportunity, and child care and development programs. Several countries have taken some steps to provide human sexuality courses for students and to provide free contraceptive information and devices and pregnancy counseling services and clinics. But from the Middle Ages on, the usual procedure for eliminating this "social ill" was to attempt to exile the prostitutes, to put them in prison, or to execute them, sometimes by decapitation.

In every city throughout the world a brothel district exists, and all the residents know where it is. Nevertheless, the authorities vigorously proclaim their moral purity, even while they are out trying to buy a young woman's favors. With this hypocritical acceptance and rejection of prostitution and prostitutes, the authorities set up the police, themselves, and the women for a complex involvement in bribes, threatened raids, and organized crime.

Every man who has trouble with a prostitute in a country in which prostitution is illegal can threaten to bring charges against her. She has no recourse, since her very existence is illegal. And the man is sure to find a sympathetic male judge. After all, it is the woman who is lustful and evil.

Governments also persecute and prosecute homosexuals. Because homosexuality is still not acceptable in the United States, nor in most Western countries, male spies will try to get a diplomat into a compromising situation vis-à-vis homosexuality and then threaten to blackmail him. Businesses will not hire homosexuals. Apartment owners will not rent to homosexuals. People will point fingers and the police will harass anyone who does not fit the expected pattern of heterosexual relationships based on the sexual definition of "manhood."

Yet, when is a sexual act a crime? The interpretations of the law by the government and by the police vary with who is involved. In 1970 a Pittsburgh paper, for example, ran a story on the arrest of a man and a woman, the man being charged "with pandering, accepting bawd money, prostitution and assignation, transporting females for the purpose of prostitution and conspiracy to commit an unlawful act." The woman was charged with "pandering, prostitution and assignation, and conspiracy to commit an unlawful act." (*Pittsburgh Press,* Oct. 25, 1970, p. 11.) Bond was set at $4,000 for the man and $2,000 for the woman.

About the same time a go-go girl (a woman with four children) was approached by a top county official in the Pittsburgh area to "turn a trick" with him. She managed to talk her way out but feared for her safety, both from government officials and from the police. This woman had become a go-go girl in order to earn enough money to feed her family. She has now, in desperation, gone on welfare to avoid the trauma of such experiences as that with the county official.

Law enforcement officials allegedly roughed up several women in New York City on April 13, 1970, who were holding a sit-in in the offices of Grove Press, protesting the degradation of women expressed in the Press's pornographic publications. Nine women were arrested and charged with "criminal trespass" and "criminal mischief."

The women were detained by the police until the following day, transferred from precinct to precinct 4 or 5 times so that their attorneys could not locate them, denied food for 14 hours (one of the women was a stress diabetic) and forced to strip and squat for the alleged purpose of searching for weapons or narcotics, although there was no narcotics or concealed weapons charge. Five of the women had their periods and were ordered to remove their tampons for the search and were refused replacements.

One of the young women refused to submit to the "strip and squat" order, which is used by some police departments to intimidate, humiliate and break down women charged with even minor offenses. Unable to cope with her, the police matrons separated her from the other women and turned her over to "the men" (male police). One of the policemen threatened "to beat her face to a pulp" if she did not submit to the police order.

Finally, a police lieutenant ordered that she be spread-eagled and shackled to the cell bars (arms and legs spread and handcuffed at the wrists and ankles) and forcibly stripped. However, the victim was simply hanged by her wrists to the cell without shackling her ankles, and stripped by two police matrons. She was not required to squat, however, so the purpose of the police treatment with respect to her was not even for illegal search but solely to punish her. (Quoted from mimeographed sheet distributed by Human Rights for Women.)

The attitudes of the society toward women define what in practice is considered a sex crime. What the police allegedly did is not considered criminal.

Rape is defined in *Webster's New Twentieth Century Dictionary* as "the crime of having sexual intercourse with a woman or girl forcibly and without her consent." Then women, by definition, are the only victims of rape. And rape is generally not taken seriously by law enforcement officials unless the woman is murdered. The rape is thought to occur because the woman "asked for it," like a robbery victim "allows" the robbery to occur. In April, 1972, an attorney in a Pittsburgh court challenged the constitutionality of the statutes dealing with prostitution because they define the sexual partner as the woman only. (*Pittsburgh Post-Gazette*, April 22, 1972.)

Recently a woman in a state capitol was raped and severely beaten, resulting in several broken bones, and the police in their questioning continually insinuated that the woman was responsible. In an unrelated meeting of state government officials where the subject of rape came up in the conversation and someone mentioned that men might get raped, the man next to me commented, "I have something to look forward to." Generally when a woman is raped, her husband becomes furious with her, not with the man.

In this attitude toward rape, women are held responsible for anything that happens to them, while at the same time they are being told that men will protect them. Women are perceived as victims or potential victims of men's actions. They are also perceived by men and women as sex objects. The reverse is not true for men. The perception frequently defines the action. Women have been so programmed into being victimized that they find it difficult to fight back, even if they do know how.

When I talked with the men in charge of physical and health education in a state department of education about the possibility of developing self-defense programs for girls and boys, I was told emphatically that girls do not need to defend themselves. Any "trouble" they may get into is of their own choosing. They get themselves into situations where they will be attacked or raped.

Marriage and divorce under state laws present a different vantage on the legality of sexual relations. Marriage makes sexual intercourse legal. Marriage also tends to make the woman a nonperson. The woman takes on the husband's name, his credit rating, his income as a measure of risk. She loses what she had gained in her "single" status. And as sexual relations become legal through marriage, so do extramarital sexual relations provide the most acceptable grounds for divorce.

With the emphasis on marriage before sexual relations and on adultery as the basis for divorce, both women and men tend to view marriage from the sexual perspective. At the same time marriage is advertised as *the* goal for women. And with the concept of marriage, in free association, runs "children." This constitutes the nuclear family—the mother at home looking after the children, keeping the home, preparing the meals, etc., while the father goes off to work. Once the woman is married and has children, her role is complicated by trying to be sexually appealing and being a "good" mother and housekeeper. The two do not mix readily.

Marriage is, then, for sex. Marriage is for procreation. The woman is sex object. The woman is mother. The woman is the earth mother, the sign of fertility, the source of life. But these are the objects of pagan worship, the attributes of evil.

These conflicts in and stratification of even the acceptable roles of women guarantee that women will bear the Traits Due to Victimization. The concept of interpersonal relationship does not appear. Marriage is a nightmare to many women and men, because they never understand themselves, and the law does not treat them, as persons, as partners, and so they never treat each other as equal persons. If marriage as an institution is to exist as a healthy growth experience for persons, those persons must be equal under the law and base their marriage on communication, understanding, love, and equality.

9. Today

Women play much the same sex roles today as they have played throughout the centuries. Little has changed. Using sexual flirtation to obtain and keep a job or a husband is almost essential. Many women marry for economic security or for power and influence. Others become mistresses to the wealthy and powerful. But probably most women, and men, marry because they are taught that this is the norm. Women are trained to see marriage and children as their lifetime goals.

Because of a lack of the understanding of interpersonal relationships and because of the rampant sexism, many young women think they have to have intercourse with every man with whom they go out. The men think they have to try "to lay" every woman with whom they go out.

The issue here is not the traditional concept of morality that sexual intercourse outside marriage is immoral and in marriage is moral, but the morality that requires respect and concern for the person. Prostitution is the mechanism to have women sexually without personal involvement. Marriage requires a long-term agreement between two persons but is usually based on the woman giving up all rights and individuality.

Church people and other guardians of public morals still easily become aroused at the evils of prostitution and righteously advocate better police action against breakers of the law. These same people, however, often support socially accepted prostitution within the bonds of marriage. Furthermore, the churches have subverted women for the support of their own programs by glorifying the traditional "mother" image, and thwarting women who seek liberation and equality.

The traditional family structure and functions, and marriage, will change if women become equal. The present use of men and women by each other will end and persons may begin to respect and "honor" each other.

CONCLUSION

Religion no longer directly dominates the political, economic, and legal power structure. Magic and witchcraft have been replaced by the physical, biological, and social sciences, except for the limited use of extrasensory perception, tarot cards, magic, readers, séances, and astrologists. The roles for women as conceived and played out in religion and witchcraft have become less directly dominant in the overall society, but the sex roles remain. Any change in women's roles, then, is going to affect most directly the attitudes toward and roles of women vis-à-vis sex.

Apparently much of the fear of the change in roles is related to the concept of woman as mother and sex object. Opposition to the women's movement, to abortion, to contraceptives, and to education in human sexuality seems to stem from this fear. The woman must retain as her primary goal motherhood and sex. She must not be equal—if society is to survive —we are told. One might ask whether a social structure that can exist only at such a cost to women should remain.

We have seen in the three sections of this book how for centuries women have been victimized and subverted, and in turn how they have developed the ego defenses of oppressed people, both extropunitive and intropunitive. Every woman in the Western world is faced today with the same dilemma that the women of the past had to face. The issue for each of us is, How am I going to deal with it?

Traditionally we respond to the world around us by reflecting and adopting the roles set out for us, including the sense of inferiority, inability, and nonpersonhood which go with them. Most probably every one of us bears one or more of the Traits Due to Victimization. Now that we know this and have seen how the victimization and subversion have worked through the centuries, we must ascertain how to end this victimization of women and how to free ourselves from the Traits Due to Victimization.

What happens to the individual affects what happens in the group, so it will probably be most helpful if we review the tendencies in behavior that the extropunitive and the intropunitive traits produce. Then we can look at the ways to overcome these with supportive assistance from the community and at the changes that must occur in the society as a whole. The women's rights movement is the catalyst both to bring women to work together and to produce radical social change.

Tendencies Produced by the Traits

EXTROPUNITIVE	INTROPUNITIVE
obsessive concern and suspicion	denial of membership in own group
slyness and cunning	withdrawal and passivity
strengthening in-group ties	clowning
prejudice against other groups	self-hate
aggression and revolt	in-group aggression
stealing	sympathy with all victims
competitiveness	symbolic status striving
rebellion	neuroticism
enhanced striving	

(Allport, p. 157.)

The tendencies of the extropunitive woman are:

1. To manipulate everyone; to become engrossed in making people do what she wants, with the *means* becoming more important than the end; to find pleasure in hearing out of another's mouth what she wants to say.
2. To assume that all other women function as she does, by never acting or speaking directly or honestly, never meaning what they say.
3. To play people off against each other through lies, suspicions, neuroses, and anxieties for the enjoyment of having such power over others.
4. To identify with a small coterie which sets itself off against all other groups and individuals.
5. To project her own guilt, frustration, and insecurity on those "outside" and hence perceived as inferior groups and individuals.
6. To put others down to increase her own self-esteem.
7. To rebel against all rules and all authority, consciously or subconsciously; to hate whatever or whoever exercises any power over her.
8. To force herself forward at whatever cost to others; to take that which is due another; to try to appear as "superwoman," to rise above all other women by manipulation, not by accomplishment.
9. To outdo whatever another person has done to *prove* she is not inferior; to be better than . . . in whatever is being measured.

The tendencies of the intropunitive woman are:

1. To hate herself.
2. To lack self-respect and self-confidence.
3. To put herself down and to expect others to put her down.

4. To laugh at herself and to expect others to laugh at her, to make jokes at her—or at women's—expense.
5. To feel insecure and incapable and so withdraw into self-pity; to want to depend on others, to act as a nonperson, but then to be frustrated by the lack of fulfillment in this role.
6. To let people do whatever they want to or with her; to assume that others rightfully have power over her because of their superiority and authority.
7. To look down on others like herself; to put them down just as she is, and expects to be, put down.
8. To be seeking praise and acceptance, especially from those whom she considers superior and so to be trying to act out her perception of what they want to see.

None of us is completely free of these tendencies, and we all know women who bear mainly the extropunitive or the intropunitive traits. We know other women who bear one or the other group of traits, depending upon the situation or their mood.

To overcome these tendencies, women can try various means as individuals. The "pull yourself up by your bootstraps" approach really doesn't work because, as we saw, the traits do not appear in a vacuum. They are the result of interaction between the woman and the world around her. Persons around the individual woman, though, can be of real help. This includes her immediate family, working associates, women in the community, and professional persons such as nonsexist psychiatrists.

There are specific things the individual woman can try to do. Each of these involves a change in the person's ego defenses, which as Traits Due to Victimization do not effectively defend and protect the ego at all. Many of the following suggestions appear to be defensive in themselves, and they are, at least until the individual reaches the point of "giving messages" that she is self-confident and secure in herself, and so not vulnerable to attempts by others to use, destroy, or laugh at her. Yet, if the victimization of women in the society continues, the new defenses will be constantly in action, for the majority of persons will have been "programmed" to expect the woman to act out the Traits Due to Victimization.

The individual woman should:

1. Think positively about herself.
2. Make herself *act* as though she has confidence in herself. Eventually after a few successes, she will begin to *feel* confident too.
3. Not let herself be used or put down. Not "give messages" that she expects to be used or put down, even though she feels weaknesses or tendencies in that direction. Try to develop a sensitive censor to such exchanges and an automatic response.
4. Try to respond to other people, men and women, as persons and treat them as such. While doing this, continue to be alert to strengths and weaknesses that affect and motivate the other person's words and actions.
5. Think of herself in terms of her abilities, her potential, and how she wants to develop these.
6. Enjoy the satisfaction of a job well done. Be able to accept praise and criticism, evaluate same, and act accordingly.
7. Differentiate between what is herself and what is the person she thinks others want to see.
8. Be as rational, honest, and direct in her interchanges with other persons as she can. Avoid manipulating people, and be aware of people trying to manipulate her.
9. Deal with her own guilt and insecurities. Not project these onto other persons and groups.

10. Accept her anxieties as such and try to work through them by using her normal patterns of action; avoid succumbing to anxieties whenever possible, and be wary of decisions and emotional responses made during spells of anxiety.

11. Not set herself up in competition with everyone. Go her own way; do as well as she can and accept that as a satisfying experience.

12. Accept her feelings and reactions. Not deny them. Bring them out into the open and deal with them.

13. Develop a life-style that provides for equality between man and woman. For example:
    a. Share the monetary costs of dates equally.
    b. Share or alternate in holding doors, coats, etc., for each other.
    c. Accept responsibility equally for looking after the children, performing household chores, washing, cooking, etc.
    d. Provide the same opportunities and support for male and female children, emphasizing the individual as opposed to the sex role. (The mother and father will serve as role models.)
    e. Make sure both parents take time off or alternate taking time from work when a baby is born, a child is ill, or an emergency arises.
    f. Retain her name and identity in marriage. Make marriage a partnership.

14. Change her vocabulary to eliminate words that convey maleness as referring to persons of both sexes, such as "chair*man*," "*man*kind," and "he" or "his" meaning "all persons."

A basic rule is that a person must love and respect and honor herself or himself to be able to love, respect, and honor others and for others to be able to love, respect, and honor her or him.

Relative success or failure in changing one's ego defenses to provide for a positive feeling and expression for one's self and toward others is highly dependent on the environment. In a situation where women are continually being treated as sex objects, laughed at, put down, and used, it is impossible for a woman to change her ego defenses successfully.

Years of training have gone into the development and maintenance of the Traits Due to Victimization in the individual woman. That many years are not available for retraining. Successful change requires a healthy, sensitive, supportive environment, hard work, and a good deal of trauma and pain. When the result can be a happier person, a person capable of interpersonal relationships—with adults and with children—a person able to maintain a steadier emotional level, the difficult times seem worthwhile.

Most women think that there is something wrong with them if they are not happy playing the role of the wife and mother, or if they cannot play these roles. Only when they realize that very few women are "happy" and feel fulfilled while limited to these roles can they throw off the feelings of guilt and self-denigration. This realization is one of the most positive results of women getting together and talking honestly with each other.

Women have been taught never to reveal their feelings. Such suppression causes women to do and say things that are "inappropriate" to the "female roles." When this happens, women feel guilty, a failure, and turn on themselves with self-chastisement, which is generally supported by the people around them—husband, children, neighbors, relatives.

Being able to talk with other women, to express anger, hostility, guilt, self-hatred, and not be judged but rather be accepted as having normal reactions in a sexist society is a gratifying experience. Women can be supportive to each other and can better understand what is happening and why by discussing common experiences and feelings.

With this support, a woman can *think* about what is going on around her, her reactions and actions, and *decide* what she wants to and can do about it, if anything.

Women in this society tend to be very lonely because of the fear of showing what they really feel and experience. They do not want to show men their "true selves" and they fear that other women will take advantage of any "weakness." Women have been trained to look down on and compete with other women. As a result, women must discuss trust and friendship frequently and openly.

With the development of the feminist movement, several different kinds of organizations have come into existence, and the kind of group an individual woman may find most interesting and helpful will depend mostly on her own needs and orientation.

1. *The consciousness-raising group* is usually a very small group of women (*or men*), no more than eight, that meets weekly simply to talk about whatever is on their minds. It is an attempt to build communication and trust in a small group which will help the individual develop the self-awareness and security that will allow her to become more self-directed. The consciousness-raising group does not act.

2. *The action or problem-solving group* is totally oriented to changing the society, to eliminating sexist practices and sex discrimination, to creating equal opportunity for women. One's consciousness gets raised by experience, but the group never sets out to work on the problems of individuals. The group may be organized to work on one specific problem such as school textbooks, athletics, etc.

3. *The self-help group* may be organized around any deficiency which the group perceives. For example, there are groups concerned with teaching auto mechanics to women, teaching women how to conduct their own pelvic examinations, teaching women how to defend themselves, teaching trades, etc.

4. *The professional group* is usually a women's caucus within a larger organization—women doctors grouping together; women historians; women in a particular church. These groups usually try to act as a pressure group to move the larger organization and to provide specific services to women. They can also be action groups geared to specific goals and can serve in consciousness-raising at least by helping women to realize that as a class they have been receiving unequal treatment in the profession. Some thirty-nine organizations concerned with the professional status of women have founded the Federation of Organizations for Professional Women.

The National Organization for Women (NOW) and Pennsylvanians for Women's Rights (PWR), for example, are more formally organized than most women's groups. Feminist groups tend to have informal structures, but both NOW and PWR and any organization covering a large geographical area have discovered that a fairly tight organization is necessary for effective functioning.

I have not mentioned the Women's Political Caucus or abortion, planned parenthood, consumer, and environment groups. All of these, in fact any organization, can be a feminist group in that its orientation is to achieve full equality between the sexes, but most of the members of these groups have not gone through the consciousness-raising process, used broadly, and so are not aware of the sexism that permeates the society, the economy, politics, education, religion, and the legal structure.

Since becoming a member of a feminist group should be a positive experience, the individual should seek out people with whom she or he can communicate or with whom she or he has common experiences. This helps in the initial adjustment to the awakening process. A consciousness-raising group can be started in a neighborhood or on the job. So can an action group. A woman may find that she wants to join a more structured group such as NOW and work on a committee dealing with a specific problem, or join a consciousness-raising group through an existing organization such as NOW or the local women's liberation group.

One must remember how crucial it is that women work together. Working together is basic to liberation from the Traits Due to Victimization. It is also essential for effective social action. We cannot make this a society in which every person can be herself or himself until we can ourselves communicate with and respect each other as persons.

Complete elimination of the Traits Due to Victimization is not possible in a sexist society. The women's rights movement, therefore, is working to change sexist systems and institutions. The movement, however, consists of members all of whom have some degree of the Traits Due to Victimization. This seems like the proverbial vicious circle. But it is clear that for major change to occur on the personal level, it must also occur on the social, and vice versa. As a result, we find in the women's movement itself women, and men, at various levels of awareness and with various motivations. Many women are trying to sort themselves out by seeking out persons going through similar experiences. Others want to change existing systems and institutions. Still others reveal predominantly extropunitive or intropunitive traits and find working for social change impossible.

The women's movement itself needs to recognize the Traits Due to Victimization and to deal with them within organizations. Women have learned to be adept at putting down other women. We all have this tendency, especially when we're trying to change, even to fight, the all-male power structure so that we can be free to be persons. We are all angry, hostile, hurt, and we are sensitive and anxious. Women's organizations must constantly evaluate themselves and their actions to know when they are succumbing to and when they are overcoming the ego defenses of oppression.

The general society must respond to the women's movement, must change, if women and men are to be free and equal in fact.

What Must Be Done

Immediately (by the present economic and political power structure)

1. Ratification of the Equal Rights Amendment.
2. Enforcement of all civil rights laws and human relations and equal pay acts that prohibit discrimination on the basis of sex in employment, education, housing, and public accommodations, both in the public and in the private sectors. Elimination of sex-segregated want ads.
3. Implementation of governmental administrative orders to end discrimination in programs receiving tax money ("contract compliance").
4. Appointment and promotion of women to at least 50 percent of government jobs at every level, including defense (again use of tax money, at least 50 percent of which comes from women).
5. Interpretation of the Fourteenth Amendment to include women of all races as persons, citizens, under the Constitution of the United States of America.

Long-Term

1. Guaranteed annual income. (1972, minimum of $6,500 for a family of four.)
2. Free food for all needy persons, including school lunches and breakfasts.
3. Adequate housing and health care.
4. Twenty-four-hour free child care and development programs in neighborhoods, housing developments, apartment houses, and industrial parks. (Use of school and church buildings for child care.)
5. Fifty percent of political candidates at every level be women.
6. Women be involved equally with men in all educational and training programs at all levels. Special efforts be made to open up traditionally male and traditionally female occupations and to equalize the pay scales. Elimination of sexism from school curricula and from the classroom.
7. Human sexuality courses be developed from the first year of school through college. Sex become an integral part of human development and maturity. Emphasis on self-perception, self-worth, development of relationships between persons. Include family planning, information on contraceptives and abortions.
8. Communications media and advertisers end the use of stereotyped roles for men and women and for sex relationships. The media need to assist in the education and liberation of persons in our society so that individuals develop the concept of freedom of choice and responsibility as an acceptable pattern for action.
9. Redefinition of manhood and womanhood as personhood. The society now expects women to act in a particular manner and men in another. Women are to carry the Traits Due

to Victimization, characteristics of an "unhealthy" person, as determined by male psychologists. Men are to be strong, physical, aggressive, ruthless, dominant. These definitions of what a person should be, determined by sex, restrict the development of both men and women as persons. Elimination of present concepts of womanhood and manhood is necessary if women and men are to be accepted as persons and allowed to develop their own abilities and potential.

What we must attain is a society in which individual persons can know and respond to other individuals as persons, where no one subverts another person. The goal, then, is for each of us to become full persons and to participate and act as such. Unless this goal is reached, "equal opportunity" only means that manipulative, oppressed women will be brought in to share the power in a society run by misogynists. Women and men must both change, and with them, the values of the society.

EPILOGUE

The moral is that, such as Nature has created her and as man actually treats her, woman is the enemy of the latter, and she can only be either a slave or a despot—never a companion. It is only when a woman becomes the equal of man by education or work, when like him she can uphold her rights, that she will be able to be a companion. As things are, we have to choose between being the anvil or the hammer.

—From H. Montgomery Hyde, *A History of Pornography,* quoting Leopold von Sacher-Masoch, *Venus in Furs.*

APPENDIX AND BIBLIOGRAPHY

APPENDIX

THE BULL OF INNOCENT VIII

Innocent, Bishop, Servant of the servants of God, for an eternal remembrance.

Desiring with the most heartfelt anxiety, even as Our Apostleship requires, that the Catholic Faith should especially in this Our day increase and flourish everywhere, and that all heretical depravity should be driven far from the frontiers and bournes of the Faithful, We very gladly proclaim and even restate those particular means and methods whereby Our pious desire may obtain its wished effect, since when all errors are uprooted by Our diligent avocation as by the hoe of a provident husbandman, a zeal for, and the regular observance of, Our holy Faith will be all the more strongly impressed upon the hearts of the faithful.

It has indeed lately come to Our ears, not without afflicting Us with bitter sorrow, that in some parts of Northern Germany, as well as in the provinces, townships, territories, districts, and dioceses of Mainz, Cologne, Treves, Salzburg, and Bremen, many persons of both sexes unmindful of their own salvation

From Montague Summers, *The Geography of Witchcraft* (University Books, Inc., 1958; second printing, 1965), pp. 533–536. All rights reserved 1965. Reprinted by arrangement with University Books, Inc.

and straying from the Catholic Faith, have abandoned themselves to devils, incubi and succubi, and by their incantations,
spells, conjurations, and other accursed charms and crafts,
enormities and horrid offences, have slain infants yet in the
mother's womb as also the offspring of cattle, have blasted the
produce of the earth, the grapes of the vine, the fruits of trees,
nay, men and women, beasts of burthen, herd-beasts, as well
as animals of other kinds, vineyards, orchards, meadows, pas-
ture-land, corn, wheat, and all other cereals; these wretches
furthermore afflict and torment men and women, beasts of
burthen, herd-beasts, as well as animals of other kinds, with
terrible and piteous pains and sore diseases, both internal and
external; they hinder men from performing the sexual act and
women from conceiving, whence husbands cannot know their
wives nor wives receive their husbands; over and above this,
they blasphemously renounce that Faith which is theirs by
the Sacrament of Baptism, and at the instigation of the Enemy
of Mankind they do not shrink from committing and perpe-
trating the foulest abominations and filthiest excesses to the
deadly peril of their own souls, whereby they outrage the Divine
Majesty and are a cause of scandal and danger to very many.
And although Our dear sons Henry Krämer and James
Sprenger, Professors of theology, of the Order of Friars Preachers, have been by Letters Apostolic delegated as Inquisitors
of these heretical pravities, and still are Inquisitors, the first in
the aforesaid parts of Northern Germany, wherein are included
those aforesaid townships, districts, dioceses, and other specified localities, and the second in certain territories which lie
along the borders of the Rhine, nevertheless not a few clerics
and lay folk of those countries, seeking too curiously to know
more than concerns them, since in the aforesaid delegatory letters there is no express and specific mention by name of these
provinces, townships, dioceses, and districts, and further since

the two delegates themselves and the abominations they are to encounter are not designated in detailed and particular fashion, these persons are not ashamed to contend with the most unblushing effrontery that these enormities are not practised in those provinces, and consequently the aforesaid Inquisitors have no legal right to exercise their powers of inquisition in the provinces, townships, dioceses, districts, and territories, which have been rehearsed, and that the Inquisitors may not proceed to punish, imprison, and penalize criminals convicted of the heinous offences and many wickednesses which have been set forth. Accordingly in the aforesaid provinces, townships, dioceses, and districts, the abominations and enormities in question remain unpunished not without open danger to the souls of many and peril of eternal damnation.

Wherefore We, as is Our duty, being wholly desirous of removing all hindrances and obstacles by which the good work of the Inquisitors may be let and tarded, as also of applying potent remedies to prevent the disease of heresy and other turpitudes diffusing their poison to the destruction of many innocent souls since Our zeal for the Faith especially incites us, lest that the provinces, townships, dioceses, districts, and territories of Germany, which We have specified, be deprived of the benefits of the Holy Office thereto assigned, by the tenour of these presents in virtue of Our Apostolic authority We decree and enjoin that the aforesaid Inquisitors be empowered to proceed to the just correction, imprisonment, and punishment of any persons, without let or hindrance, in every way as if the provinces, townships, dioceses, districts, territories, yea, even the persons and their crimes in this kind were named and particularly designated in Our letters. Moreover, for greater surety We extend these letters deputing this authority to cover all the aforesaid provinces, townships, dioceses, districts, and territories, persons, and crimes newly rehearsed, and We grant permission to the aforesaid Inquisitors, to one separately or to both, as also to Our dear son John Gremper, priest of the diocese of Constance, Master of Arts, their notary, or to any other public notary, who shall be by them, or by one of them, temporarily delegated to those provinces, townships, dioceses, districts, and aforesaid territories, to proceed, according to the regulations of the Inquisition, against any persons of whatsoever rank and high estate, correcting, mulcting, imprisoning, punishing, as their crimes merit, those whom they have found guilty, the penalty being adapted to the offence. Moreover they shall enjoy a full and perfect faculty of expounding and preaching the word of God to the faithful, so often as opportunity may offer and it may seem good to them, in each and every parish church of the said provinces, and they shall freely and lawfully perform any rites or execute any business which may appear advisable in the aforesaid cases. By Our supreme authority We grant them anew full and complete faculties.

At the same time by Letters Apostolic We require Our venerable Brother, the Bishop of Strasburg [Albrecht von Bayern, 1478–1506], that he himself shall announce, or by some other or others cause to be announced the burthen of Our Bull, which he shall solemnly publish when and so often as he deems it necessary, or when he shall be requested so to do by the Inquisitors or by one of them. Nor shall he suffer them in disobedience to the tenour of these presents to be molested or hindered by any authority whatsoever, but he shall threaten all who endeavour to hinder or harass the Inquisitors, all who oppose them, all rebels, of whatsoever rank, estate, position, pre-eminence, dignity, or any condition they may be, or whatsoever privilege of exemption they may claim, with excommunication, suspension, interdict, and yet more terrible penalties, censures, and punishment, as may seem good to him, and that without any right of appeal, and if he will he may by Our authority aggravate and renew these penalties as often as he list, calling in, if so please him, the help of the secular arm.

Non obstantibus . . . Let no man therefore . . . But if any dare to do so, which God forbid, let him know that upon him will fall the wrath of Almighty God, and of the Blessed Apostles Peter and Paul.

Given at Rome, at S. Peter's, on the 9 December of the Year of the Incarnation of Our Lord one thousand four hundred and eighty-four, in the first Year of Our Pontificate.

BIBLIOGRAPHY

INTRODUCTION

Allport, Gordon W., *The Nature of Prejudice*. Doubleday Anchor Book, 1958.

Section I. THE SUBJUGATION OF WOMEN: A JUDEO-CHRISTIAN TRADITION

Albright, William Foxwell, *From the Stone Age to Christianity: Monotheism and the Historical Process*, Second Edition. The Johns Hopkins Press, 1957.

Barry, Colman J., O.S.B. (ed.), *Readings in Church History*, Vols. I, II, III. The Newman Press, 1960 (I), 1965 (II, III).

Culver, Elsie, *Women in the World of Religion*. Doubleday & Company, Inc., 1967.

Daly, Mary, *The Church and the Second Sex*. Harper & Row, Publishers, Inc., 1968.

de Vaux, Roland, *Ancient Israel: Its Life and Institutions*, tr. by John McHugh. McGraw-Hill Book Co., Inc., 1961.

Genesis III, Vols. 1 and 2. Philadelphia Task Force on Women in Religion, P.O. Box 24003, Philadelphia, Pa. 19139.

John XXIII, Pope, *Mater et Magistra: Christianity and Social Progress*, tr. by William J. Gibbons, S.J. The Paulist Press, 1961.

McGrath, Sister Albertus Magnus, *What a Modern Catholic Believes About Women*. Thomas More, 1972.

Monday Morning, A Magazine for Presbyterian Ministers, Vol. 37, No. 14 (July, 1972).

Morris, Joan, "Women and Episcopal Power," *New Blackfriars,* Vol. 53, No. 623 (May, 1972), pp. 205–210.

Second Vatican Council, *Pastoral Constitution on the Church in the Modern World.* December 7, 1965. Washington, D.C.: National Catholic Welfare Conference.

Seltman, Charles, *Women in Antiquity.* Collier Books, 1962.

Sitwell, Sacheverell, *Monks, Nuns and Monasteries.* Holt, Rinehart & Winston, Inc., 1965.

Section II. WITCHCRAFT:
A THREAT TO CHURCH AND STATE SUPREMACY

Baroja, Julio Caro, *The World of the Witches,* tr. by O. N. V. Glendinning. The University of Chicago Press, 1965.

Cohn, Norman, *The Pursuit of the Millennium.* Essential Books, Inc., 1957.

de Plancy, Collin, *Dictionary of Witchcraft,* ed. and tr. by Wade Baskin. Philosophical Library, Inc., 1965.

Douglas, Mary (ed.), *Witchcraft, Confessions & Accusations.* London: Tavistock Publications, Ltd., 1970.

Glanvill, Joseph, *Saducismus Triumphatus: Or, Full and Plain Evidence Concerning Witches and Apparitions (1689).* Facsimile reproduction with an introduction by Coleman O. Parsons. Gainesville, Florida: Scholars' Facsimiles & Reprints, 1966.

Glass, Justine, *They Foresaw the Future: The Story of Fulfilled Prophecy.* G. P. Putnam's Sons, Inc., 1969.

Hansen, Chadwick, *Witchcraft at Salem.* The New American Library of World Literature, Inc., 1969.

Hansen, Joseph, *Quellen und Untersuchungen zur Geschichte des Hexenwahns und der Hexenverfolgungen im Mittelalter.* Bonn: C. Georgi, 1901.

———— *Zauberwahn, Inquisition, und Hexenprozess im Mittelalter und die Entstehung der grossen Hexenverfolgung.* Munich (Leipzig): Oldenbourg, 1900.

Lea, Henry Charles (comp.), *Materials Toward a History of Witchcraft,* arr. and ed. by Arthur C. Howland. 3 vols. University of Pennsylvania Press, 1939.

Le Roy Ladurie, Emmanual, *Les Paysans de Languedoc.* Paris: Éditions S.E.V.P.E.N., 1966.

Macfarlane, Alan, *Witchcraft in Tudor and Stuart England: A Regional and Comparative Study*. London: Routledge & Kegan Paul, Ltd., 1970.

Malleus Maleficarum, tr. with an Introduction, Bibliography, and Notes by Montague Summers. London: The Pushkin Press, 1948.

Michelet, Jules, *Satanism and Witchcraft: A Study in Medieval Superstition*, tr. by A. R. Allinson. Citadel Press, 1939.

Monter, E. William (ed.), *European Witchcraft*. John Wiley & Sons, Inc., 1969.

Notestein, Wallace, *A History of Witchcraft in England from 1558 to 1718*. Washington: American Historical Association, 1911.

Peel, Edgar, and Southern, Pat, *The Trials of the Lancashire Witches: A Study of Seventeenth-Century Witchcraft*. Taplinger Publishing Company, Inc., 1969.

Rose, Elliot, *A Razor for a Goat: A Discussion of Certain Problems in the History of Witchcraft and Diabolism*. Toronto: University of Toronto Press, 1962.

Rosen, George, "A Study of the Persecution of Witches in Europe as a Contribution to the Understanding of Mass Delusions and Psychic Epidemics," *Journal of Health & Human Behavior*, I (1960), pp. 200–211.

Russell, Jeffrey Burton, *Witchcraft in the Middle Ages*. Cornell University Press, 1972.

Seebohm, Frederic, *The Era of the Protestant Revolution*. AMS Press, Inc., 1971. Reprint of 1903 Second Edition.

Summers, Montague, *The Geography of Witchcraft*. University Books, Inc., 1958.

Thorndike, Lynn, *A History of Magic and Experimental Science*. 8 vols. The Macmillan Company, 1923–1958.

The Trial of Joan of Arc. Being the verbatim report of the proceedings from the Orleans Manuscript, tr. with an Intro. and notes by W. S. Scott. London: Folio Society, Inc., 1956.

Wedeck, Harry E., *Treasury of Witchcraft*. Philosophical Library, Inc., 1961.

Williams, George Huntston (ed.), *Spiritual and Anabaptist Writers*. The Library of Christian Classics, Vol. XXV. The Westminster Press, 1957.

"Witches and the Community: An Anthropological Approach to the History of Witchcraft," *Times Literary Supplement*, No. 3 (October 30, 1970), p. 583.

Section III. Sex:
The Self-destructive Weapon

Adler, Polly, *A House Is Not a Home*. Rinehart & Company, Inc., 1950.

Barlay, Stephen, *Sex Slavery: A Documentary Report on the International Scene Today*. London: William Heinemann, Ltd., 1968.

Bell, Ernest A., *White Slavery Today*. Chicago: Lincoln W. Walter, 1917.

Benjamin, Harry, and Masters, R. E. L., *Prostitution and Morality*. The Julian Press, Inc., 1964.

Bishop, Lloyd O., and DeLoach, Will S., "Marie Meurdrac—First Lady of Chemistry?" *Journal of Chemical Education*, Vol. 47, No. 6 (June, 1970), pp. 448–449.

Flexner, Abraham, *Prostitution in Europe*. New York: Century, 1914.

Greenwald, Harold, *The Call Girl: A Social and Psychoanalytic Study*. Ballantine Books, Inc., 1958.

Herold, J. Christopher, *Love in Five Temperaments*. Atheneum Publishers, 1961.

Hyde, H. Montgomery, *A History of Pornography*. Farrar, Straus & Giroux, Inc., 1965.

Marcus, Steven, *The Other Victorians: A Study of Sexuality and Pornography in Mid-Nineteenth-Century England*. Basic Books, Inc., 1966.

Olsen, Jack, *The Girls in the Office*. Simon & Schuster, Inc., 1972.

Perrin, Noel, *Dr. Bowdler's Legacy: A History of Expurgated Books in England and America*. Atheneum Publishers, 1969.

Report of the Joint Task Force on Sexism in Education. 1972. Available from the Secretary of Education, Department of Education, Harrisburg, Pa.

Scott, Benjamin, *A State Iniquity: Its Rise, Extension, and Overthrow*. Augustus M. Kelley, 1968. Reprint of 1890 edition.

Vernon, Virginia, *Enchanting Little Lady: The Criminal Life of the Marquise de Brinvilliers*. Abelard-Schuman, Limited, 1964.

Vice Commission of Chicago, *The Social Evil in Chicago: A Study of Existing Conditions*. Chicago: Gunthorp Warren Co., 1911.